GREATNESS IN THE WHITE HOUSE

ROBERT K. MURRAY AND TIM H. BLESSING

GREATNESS

—— IN THE ——

WHITE HOUSE

RATING THE PRESIDENTS

Second, Updated Edition

*From George Washington Through
Ronald Reagan*

The Pennsylvania State University Press, University Park, Pennsylvania

Library of Congress Cataloging-in-Publication Data

Murray, Robert K.
    Greatness in the White House : rating the presidents / Robert K. Murray and Tim H.
Blessing. — 2nd updated ed.
            p.   cm.
    "From George Washington through Ronald Reagan."
    Includes bibliographical references and index.
    ISBN 0-271-01089-4 (alk. paper). — ISBN 0-271-01090-8 (pbk.)
    1. Presidents—United States—Rating of.   2. United States—Politics and
government.   I. Blessing, Tim H.   II. Title.
E176.1.M955   1993
353.03'1'0922—dc20   93–20451
                                                                          CIP

Published by The Pennsylvania State University Press,
Suite C, Barbara Building, University Park, PA 16802-1003

It is the policy of The Pennsylvania State University Press to use acid-free paper for the first
printing of all clothbound books. Publications on uncoated stock satisfy the minimum
requirements of American National Standard for Information Sciences—Permanence of Paper
for Printed Library Materials, ANSI Z39.48–1984.

Contents

Preface to the Second, Updated Edition

Greatness in the White House was originally published in 1988 as *No. 50* in The Pennsylvania State University Studies series. It was included in the series and was set up in camera-ready copy by computer in order to keep printing costs low and to facilitate the speed with which the results of the Presidential Performance Study could be placed in the hands of the many historians and others who had helped us with the presidential survey.

It was our expectation that this would suffice, but the demand for the survey's results exceeded both our expectations and those of the Pennsylvania State University Press. Not only American historians but also journalists, psychologists, sociologists, political scientists, and numerous nonprofessionals requested and purchased copies.

While this original printing was being depleted, we were engaged with a group of American historians in a modest follow-up study involving the Reagan years. Undertaken without any thought that it would be worth more than an interesting article, we planned to write up the results in that format. At the same time, we were continually receiving reactions to the 1988 survey—a few critical, but most favorable—which included numerous requests that we expand our original survey results to incorporate a ranking of the Reagan administration.

The confluence of several events was suddenly fortuitous. The original 1988 survey edition was rapidly running out, Penn State Press had decided to reissue the 1988 survey in standard book format, and our Reagan study had just been completed and was being prepared for publication.

The result is the product before you. It contains the original text (revised and updated) and all the charts from the 1988 survey (except for some of the original survey's raw scores) and now also includes the most recent assessment of the Reagan years by almost five hundred American historians, along with the necessary corroborative survey data and information.

We trust that this new edition will serve as useful a purpose as the first, and be as widely accepted. If nothing else, it should continue to stimulate debate about what constitutes greatness in the White House.

State College, Pa.   *Robert K. Murray*
Summer 1993   *Tim H. Blessing*

Preface and Acknowledgments

In a project of this nature, the number of persons to be thanked is legion. No reasonable amount of space would permit even the mere listing of the names of those who contributed to this presidential performance study in one way or another. We are especially grateful to the sixty interviewees who spent hours in verbal discourse with us and to the nearly one thousand American historians who took the time to answer our survey questionnaires and return them for analysis. Without the cooperation of these historians, this study would have been impossible.

Apart from these two historian groups, there are a few specific individuals who have our heartfelt thanks. Professor Stanley Weintraub, Director of the Institute for the Arts and Humanistic Studies, and Dr. Stanley Paulson, former Dean of the College of Liberal Arts at The Pennsylvania State University, gave psychological and monetary support throughout the period required to secure the data. Robert D. Lee, Director for Research in the Institute of Public Administration, and Robert Mowitz (now deceased), Director of the Institute of Public Administration at The Pennsylvania State University, provided advice on sampling techniques and supplied us with specialized personnel to help construct the survey instrument and solve polling problems as they arose. Glen Kreider, Research Application Specialist, and William McCane, Instructional Specialist, both in the Center for Computer Assistance at The Pennsylvania State University, were our contacts for computer-related problems. Historians Philip S. Klein, Warren W. Hassler, Ira V. Brown, Earl Kaylor, and Richard Hatch gave unselfishly of their time to aid us with the historical aspects of the study.

The laborious chores of envelope stuffing, mail sorting, and codification of data would never have been completed without the help of such persons as Robin Floyd, Janet Winters, Kathy Cresswell, Richard Russell, Michael Pavkovic, Su-Ya Chang, Joshua Rosen, and Marilyn Parrish. Shirley Rader, Jan Shoemaker, and especially Carol McGahen cheerfully assumed the burden of typing the manuscript and setting up the many tables and appendixes. Eve Murray's editorial and literary suggestions made the conversion of statistical data into prose read less boring than it might otherwise have been.

The main purpose of the following narrative is to describe this presidential performance project from the beginning and to define and analyze the major results. Although this whole procedure involved many people and by its nature was a joint enterprise, we must accept the sole responsibility for the final interpretations placed on the assembled data and for the general conclusions which we believe the data suggested. We hope these are accurate and represent fairly the attitudes of the survey respondents and the interviewees who participated. If not, the fault is ours alone.

Robert K. Murray
Tim H. Blessing

Introduction

THE PRESIDENCY AND A SUCCESSFUL performance in that office have for years been subjects for analysis and scrutiny. From the time of the Constitutional Convention to the present, no aspect of our governmental system has occasioned more comment or controversy. The presidency has been our most centralized and celebrated governmental institution, and in the popular mind, at least, has been the preeminent federal agency for good or ill. Indeed, history shows that this uniquely American creation—the presidency—has at times been both a bane and a blessing for the American democratic experience.

In recent years a number of scholars have formulated theories about and created models for the presidency. Regarding the office as a critical litmus test for the successful operation of American government, they have written treatises dissecting presidential custodianship. Political scientists such as Richard E. Neustadt and Thomas E. Cronin have examined the case of strong and aggressive presidents like Franklin Roosevelt, claiming that the actions of these chief executives have given rise to a so-called textbook model of the presidency. Such a president's actions, the theory goes, serve objectives far beyond his party's and his own. In this view the president is seen as being the necessary catalyst for progress in both the domestic and foreign field; only he can be the architect of public policy and move the nation forward; he alone can draw the nation together and provide confidence and moral leadership. And if he is successful, all will be well with the nation. Professor Neustadt has put it bluntly: "What is good for the country is good for the president, and vice versa."[1]

This view of the presidency has helped spawn an awe of the office, and that awe has survived despite the damaging impact of Vietnam and Watergate. Sidney Hyman, a political historian, has stated that the president "is the one common reference point from which we take our bearings as a people."[2] In a sense, the president has become our "elected king," but in another sense he has also remained our intimate. No matter how we try, the president, as Professor Neustadt has claimed, "seeps irrepressibly into our hearts. He dwells in us. We cannot keep him out."[3] Professor Clinton Rossiter, another analyst of the "textbook" presidency, admitted that there is a "feeling of veneration, if not exactly reverence," for the authority and dignity of the office and once described Lincoln as "the martyred Christ of democracy's passion play."[4]

It is little wonder that this office also attracted the attention of political scientists, sociologists, psychologists, and social psychologists who are primarily interested in assessing and defining the elusive qualities of "leadership." Although leadership has been one of the oldest and most critically examined aspects of personality, these scholars believe that too little research has been done on the specific subject of *political* leadership. As for *presidential* leadership, articles and monographs have begun to appear, most of them involving complicated quantitative analyses. Evaluating such variables as "presidential age," "previous political experience," "relationships with Congress and the courts," and so on, these studies have sought not only to pinpoint presidential leadership qualities but also to define the various components of the presidency and to discover the key ingredients in presidential success.[5]

Two of the main hallmarks of this "new" presidential scholarship have been an ever-increasing sophistication in methodology and subtlety in analysis. For instance, Professor Kristen Monroe has taken the common perception that presidential popularity and American economic welfare are entwined and used it as a tool to explain on a deeper level the linkages between the collective consciousness of the American people and their physical and fiscal well-being.[6] In her *Presidential Popularity and the Economy*, she traces the ebb and flow of presidential popularity from 1965 to 1980 and measures how it corresponded to the degree of health of the nation's economy. As with most of the new presidential scholars, Monroe did not stop with simply establishing a correlative figure between economic ebbs and flows and the changes in public appraisals of the incumbent; instead she fine-tuned the figures by examining such variables as the expectations people hold for the two political parties in economic matters (Republican presidents and Democratic presidents are held to very different standards), the various political allegiances of the voters, the impact of political events (such as scandals), group identifications and dynamics, and other "noneconomic" inputs. Professor Monroe concluded her study by constructing a "popularity" model which she claimed contained the major factors that mediate and modify the effects of economic events on a president's public standing.[7]

While studies such as Professor Monroe's explore the presidency and its interaction with one particular environment, other studies, such as those by Professors George C. Edwards and Stephen J. Wayne, have attempted to examine the presidency by probing a number of diverse matters—public and media interaction, presidential decision-making, budgetary and economic policy planning, foreign and defense policy concerns, and executive policy implementation. At the heart of the Edwards-Wayne work is an attempt to clarify and sharpen the questions we have asked about the presidency, to define and delimit the terms used to examine the office as a whole, and to find objective measures and quantifiable data to shape the answers given.[8]

This present study, the Murray-Blessing survey, is an attempt to approach many of these same problems, but from a somewhat different set of perspectives. Social scientists have long recognized that any judgment in a social science field is colored by a degree of subjectivity. We therefore decided to test some of the testers of the presidency, turning the spotlight around for a moment on certain of those who have traditionally played a crucial role in examining that office—American historians. Indeed, of all the academic groups interested in the presidency, none has so persistently followed its development or chartered its ups and downs as American historians. Deeply steeped in the details of the American past, they have long regarded the presidency as one of the most important factors in influencing the course of the nation's history. History itself seems to agree by allowing the American experience to be most easily divided into presidential years and administrations.[9]

To historians, perhaps more than to political scientists or other scholars, the presidency appears as *both* an institution and an individual. Not only do these two components of the presidency exist side by side, but each is molded by and dependent on the other. As a result, in the historians' minds there is a blending of the interaction between them and of the impossibility of evaluating the one without the other. Historians admit that presidential models are important and that studies of generic presidential qualities contribute to a general understanding of the office. But historians have to grapple with the fact that the presidency is never held in a vacuum and that each holder of the office has been himself unique.

Along with other presidential scholars, historians concede that the presidency is an underdefined institution. It is unclear what precisely is expected of it. The Constitution is not much help. Article II states in its important parts:

> The executive Power shall be vested in a President. . . . He shall hold his Office during the Term of four years. . . . No person except a natural born Citizen . . . shall be eligible to the Office of President; neither shall any Person be eligible to that Office who shall not have attained to the Age of Thirty-five years, and been fourteen years a resident within the United States.

As for presidential powers and duties, Article II specifies that the president shall preserve, protect, and defend the Constitution of the United States, act as commander-in-chief, grant reprieves and pardons, make treaties, nominate diplomatic officers and Supreme Court judges, secure written reports from the various heads of departments, call special sessions of Congress, recommend legislation, receive foreign emissaries, and execute all laws.

Despite a lack of precise criteria and the ambiguous nature of the office, historians, either explicitly or implicitly in their classroom lectures and in their writings, have passed judgment on the men who have held the presidency, building up a huge literature on individual presidential performances in the process. This literature provides the basis for most other presidency scholarship. Political scientists, sociologists, and psychologists, even after creating their models and employing their sophisticated quantitative techniques, have cross-related their results concerning presidential performance or success to traditional historical verdicts, declaring their findings or their theories "reliable" if the two matched.[10]

As yet no study has appeared either to validate or refute the judgment of American historians on the presidents. Ironically, historians have not taken their own collective opinion as seriously as have many of their nonhistorian colleagues. The diversity of presidential situations, the different personalities involved, the complexity of issues and their solutions, the imponderability of the impact of future events, and the suspicion that historians themselves are subject to the biases of contemporary culture make grading presidents appear somewhat frivolous and futile to them. Ranking presidential performances is, as historian Bert Cochran once said, "to reduce history to a parlor game."[11] But parlor game or not, the opinions held by historians about past presidents have conditioned the academic and the non-academic world alike to view presidential performances in a particular way and have supplied the guidelines by which contemporary and future presidents are likely to be judged.

Who, then, are these men and women upon whom presidential reputations come to rest and who set the parameters, if not the substance, of much presidential research? What are their specific views of the office and of the men who have held it? And considering their own backgrounds, biases, and personalities, are their judgments *really* worthy of such widespread acceptance?

O N E

A Game for All Seasons: Past Presidential Polls

PROFESSIONAL INTEREST IN RATING the presidents dates from the Arthur M. Schlesinger, Sr., poll of 1948.[1] A history professor at Harvard University, Professor Schlesinger solicited the views of fifty-five "experts," most of whom were historians. The findings were subsequently published in *Life* magazine and were immediately accepted by the press as representing the collective judgment of historians everywhere.[2] Fourteen years later Schlesinger repeated the exercise, this time surveying seventy-five "experts." Fifty-eight were historians (including most of those polled in 1948), with the remainder being mainly journalists and political scientists.[3] Published in the *New York Times Magazine*, the results of this poll reenforced those of the earlier one and even more firmly established the Schlesinger findings as the common verdict of the historical fraternity. In both polls, the top five presidents, in descending order, were Abraham Lincoln, George Washington, Franklin D. Roosevelt, Woodrow Wilson, and Thomas Jefferson. The bottom two were Ulysses S. Grant and Warren G. Harding.[4]

The procedures used in the Schlesinger polls of 1948 and 1962 were extremely simple. All presidents who had served any appreciable time in office were listed (excluding Harry S. Truman in 1948 but including Dwight D. Eisenhower in 1962). William H. Harrison and James A. Garfield were omitted from both polls because of their brief tenures. Each respondent was asked to place after the president's name the letter A, B, C, D, or E, signifying Great, Near Great, Average, Below Average, or Failure. In true academic fashion, they were allowed to shade their evaluation if they so desired by adding a plus or a minus sign. "The test in each case," read the instructions, was "performance in office, omitting everything done before or after."[5] Aside from this requirement, the respondents were left to apply whatever criteria they wanted.

Although these two Schlesinger polls were given immediate public credence, many historians were doubtful about the validity of the rankings. Schlesinger himself held no brief for his methodology and intended the results to represent only a "highly informed opinion" by a blue-ribbon group of citizens. Flaws did exist in the Schlesinger procedures, and Stanford historian Thomas A. Bailey in *Presidential Greatness* (1966) pinpointed most of them. Professor Bailey contended that the political bias of the Schlesinger respondents was clearly pro-Democratic and economically liberal (Democrats did outnumber Republicans two to one). For the most part, the respondents were born in the North and came mainly from the Northeast, the Middle Atlantic states, and the upper Midwest. The majority possessed Ph.D.'s from New England universities, half of the group having some sort of academic connection with Harvard. All were published scholars or writers—half being authors of well-known college or secondary school texts. Teaching historians, as contrasted to publishing historians, were excluded; no women were in the sample; the southern area of the nation was ignored; and there was no representation by ethnic or racial groups.[6]

Professor Bailey's book not only criticized the composition of the Schlesinger samples but also pointed up the general pitfalls inherent in rating presidents. While not providing answers, Professor Bailey asked such pertinent questions as: How much of the respondents' evaluations rested on presidential physical appearances and charisma? How much did "the times" make the man? Was it important to the ranking process that some presidents were applauded by the contemporary press while others were castigated by it? Did the shifting winds of public opinion on issues (one decade, civil rights; another decade, concern for the economy or war) cause the judgment of historians about presidents to be as much visceral as cerebral?

Although believing such questions to be largely unanswerable and stating bluntly that ranking presidents was an ill-fated attempt to "measure the immeasurable," Professor Bailey nonetheless proceeded to draw up thirty-five major and eight minor tests that he thought should be applied to each president. These ranged from assessing the kind of personal enemies a president had made to evaluating the type of world leadership he had offered.[7] However, when Professor Bailey applied as many of these yardsticks to each president as he could, he arrived at almost the same conclusions the two Schlesinger polls did. He juggled slightly the standings of such presidents as John Adams, Jefferson, Jackson, Polk, Truman, Cleveland, and Buchanan, but he agreed that the three foremost presidents in the nation's history were indeed Lincoln, Washington, and Franklin Roosevelt.[8]

Other attempts at rating the presidents followed despite the known difficulties. In 1977 the United States Historical Society asked the heads of one hundred history departments to name the ten "greatest" presidents. When the responses of the eighty-five who replied were tabulated, Lincoln, Washington, and Franklin Roosevelt again headed the list. Lincoln received a unanimous vote of eighty-five; Washington received eighty-four and Franklin Roosevelt eighty-one. Next in line came Theodore Roosevelt (79), Jefferson (78), Wilson (74), Jackson (73), Truman (64), Polk (38), and John Adams (35). These ten names (although not in this exact order) were the same ones that appeared at the top of the Schlesinger list in 1962.[9]

Four years later, in 1981, David L. Porter, a historian at William Penn College, asked forty-one colleagues whom he handpicked to rate the presidents. This respondent group, like Schlesinger's, had impeccable scholarly reputations, being known primarily for their writings. They once again selected Lincoln, Washington, and Franklin Roosevelt as the top three. Because of its later date, the Porter poll contained presidents the 1962 Schlesinger poll had not included—John F. Kennedy, Lyndon Johnson, Richard Nixon, and Gerald Ford. Of these four, Johnson was ranked the highest (Near Great), with Nixon being banished to the failing group to join Grant and Harding.[10]

The very next year, 1982, Steve Neal, a political reporter for the *Chicago Tribune*, tried his hand at rating presidents by querying forty-nine "leading historians and political scholars" (all of whom had published a biography or some seminal work on a president) for their views. Four of these forty-nine had also taken part in the original Schlesinger survey almost thirty-four years before.[11] Neal's respondents were asked to rate the presidents on a scale of 0 to 5 in five categories (leadership, accomplishments, political skill, appointments, and character) and also, separately, to list the ten "best" and the ten "worst" presidents in history. The results were slightly confusing. The point totals of the five categories made Franklin Roosevelt second only to Lincoln, but on the list of the ten "best" he was ranked as third behind Washington. Nixon, in turn, was fourth from the bottom in the five-category point totals but was ranked next to last, just above Harding, in the ten "worst" group.[12]

By 1982, rating the presidents was nothing new. A perennial interest in doing so persisted even though the results were not that surprising or novel. The continuing need for contemporary presidents to be added to the list stimulated a recurring desire to measure these newcomers against presidents of the past. Still, the original shortcomings of the Schlesinger polls continued to cast doubt on the results. None of the polls since 1948 attempted to define or uncover specific criteria for evaluating presidential performances. All the polls involved only a handful of historians, selected mainly from the "elite" of the profession with an emphasis on publications and membership in the faculties of the "top" institutions. Also, none of the polls attempted to examine the relationship between the respondents' rankings and such variables as the respondents' gender and age, residence, place of birth, source and type of education, historical specialty, and so on. As a result, the rating of presidents remained for most historians just a game, and a suspect game at that.

T W O

The Murray-Blessing Ratings

A NEW AND DIFFERENT PRESIDENTIAL survey was initiated in 1982 when we sent 1,997 questionnaires to all Ph.D.-holding American historians with the rank of assistant professor or above listed in the American Historical Association's *Guide to Departments of History* for 1979–1980 and 1980–1981.[1] The decision to use this particular group of historians was dictated by survey costs, by the high level of these historians' training, and by the fact that they were all involved in full-time teaching (administrators and those with joint appointments in other departments were excluded). That this group was in daily contact with students and was influencing students' opinions was considered important.

Broader in scope than previous polling efforts, this survey was undertaken to meet some of the criticisms leveled at the other polls. In developing the study and forming a survey instrument, advice was secured from psychologists, public administration personnel, political scientists, and opinion-gathering specialists. Modern opinion research procedures were followed, and the mainframe computer at The Pennsylvania State University was used to assess the results. Preliminary interviews with a small group of historians and a field-testing program were used to validate the pertinence of the survey questions and of the information sought. The ultimate goal was not only to determine once again the attitude of historians toward various presidential performances but also to discover, if possible, the reasons historians considered some presidents superior to others.

This attempt to "measure the immeasurable" early confronted the problem of proper yardsticks. At first adopting Professor Bailey's forty-three tests, we soon discovered that there was as much controversy among historians about the tests' validity as there was about their applicability to given presidential administrations. Besides, using forty-three tests for thirty-six presidential performances (excluding William H. Harrison, Garfield, and Reagan) quickly produced such an unintelligible jumble that it was impossible to come to any conclusions. Other tests we subsequently devised proved equally faulty. At one point we decided to allow each respondent to set his own criteria but have him or her explain precisely what they were. This resulted in mainly vague and general statements that were largely unrevealing. In the end a much more difficult course was decided upon—to supply or ask for no criteria, but to construct a system of cross-referenced questions about the presidency and about specific presidential actions that, when compared and analyzed, might disclose the hidden and often unarticulated criteria by which historians actually judge presidential performances.

The result was a nineteen-page 180-question survey package that required more than an hour to complete if taken seriously. This caused us concern because of what such a burden might do to the response rate. To be regarded as trustworthy, a mail survey, if used alone, should have at least a 50 percent return. But studies have shown that no poll longer than twelve pages could be expected to have more than a 65 percent response and that if a questionnaire went over twelve pages or 125 questions the return rate would drop below that figure drastically.[2] Our survey did both, and beside being nineteen pages long the 180 questions required almost 400 separate responses by each historian. Moreover, our own preliminary interviews had uncovered considerable animosity among historians for "computer-connected" projects, and we feared that this attitude might also cause a weak return and prejudice the validity of any findings. Indeed, one test poll we conducted showed that more than 70 percent of the historians we questioned disapproved to one degree or another of the use of quantification and computers in history. Hence, even before the survey instrument was sent out to the general sample, we decided to evaluate the effect of any such nonresponse by conducting an oral in-depth survey of sixty historians, chosen at random, using face-to-face interviews.[3]

In these interviews, the selected historians were encouraged to elaborate on their answers to the survey's questions as much as they wished. In fact, for certain predesignated questions, the interviewer actively solicited both general and detailed responses. These "probe" questions were designed to encourage the historians to reflect on their own reasoning on certain crucial points and to report their reflections to the interviewer.

Once the test surveys and these face-to-face interviews were completed, the mail survey was sent out, and upon its return the reconciliation of the data was begun. Our first discovery was that the results of all three investigative phases did not differ more than would be expected through random scattering: the presidents were similarly ranked, and the cross-referenced questions showed similar response patterns. While the oral interviews gave us valuable insights into historians' thinking about the presidency, the mail survey permitted a much better tracking of the total response by the historical profession. The mail survey, moreover, permitted a much better tracking of several groups of historians whose opinions differed somewhat from the mainstream.

Section I of the mail survey asked the respondents for certain personal information, such as date and state of birth, years and institutions of advanced degrees, areas of concentration (historical time period), subject matter specialty, number of students taught per year, and number and type of publications. Section II, containing sixty-seven questions, requested the respondents' views on the presidential office in general. Section III, comprising 113 questions, asked for the respondents' reactions to specific presidential actions in three time periods: from 1789 to 1865, from 1865 to 1945, and since 1945. Finally, Section IV requested that the respondents rank all presidents (except for William H. Harrison, James Garfield, and Ronald Reagan) within the general categories of Great, Near Great, Above Average, Average, Below Average, and Failure (see sample survey questionnaire in Appendix 1).

By the summer of 1982, there were 846 completed questionnaires in hand, and the laborious coding of the information was begun. While this coding was being completed, 107 additional questionnaires were received. These were processed separately, their rankings compared with the 846 already coded and found not to be significantly different. Seventeen other questionnaires received were missing a page or otherwise incomplete. Although this reply rate of 48.6 percent (970) represented very nearly half the total mailed and was a response beyond our expectations, we had been wise in having already incorporated into the project the random-sampling interviews that could now supply a safeguard and provide a check on the mail survey's reliability.

Reaction to the mail survey by the historians ranged from praise to condemnation. Thirteen letters and comments on sixteen questionnaires applauded the study, maintaining that it was worthwhile and well constructed. Eleven other letters and comments on twenty-six questionnaires saw the matter differently. "I feel uncomfortable with rank-order polls and computer studies of this sort" was a common remark. Several respondents stated that the questionnaire was misleading and a waste of everybody's time. One wrote that if historians possessed a monitoring organization like physicians had in the AMA, he would have us up on charges of incompetency. Perhaps the most cutting remark came from one historian who said he was not returning the questionnaire because "I plan to have it copied and examined by my graduate students, who may, I fear, be tempted into similar activities unless forewarned by this example."

As in the face-to-face interviews (where only a few objections to the study surfaced), the vast majority of those responding did not comment one way or the other and evidently participated in good faith. No remarks appeared on 897 questionnaires, but on seventy-three questionnaires a word, short phrase, or question mark did sometimes pop up to indicate the respondent's displeasure with a particular question. Among the seventeen questionnaires returned incomplete, four were left blank with appended notes stating that the recipient did not wish to be involved in any study attempting to rank the presidents. Several "experts" whom Schlesinger had first approached in 1948 and 1962 had also refused to participate in his polls for the same reason.[4]

An analysis of Section I of the first 846 surveys subjected to the coding and cross-referencing process showed that 783 respondents were male, 59 were female, and 4 did not indicate gender. Grouped by age, 23 respondents were 29 to 34 years of age, 302 were 35 to 44, 296 were 45 to 54, 173 were 55 to 64, 49 were 65 or older, and 3 did not report their ages. The place of birth of respondents ranged from a high of 108 for New York to 0 for Alaska, Hawaii, Nevada, New Hampshire, and Wyoming. The number of respondents born in Illinois (52) and Ohio (51) were next in line to the number born in the Empire State.[5]

For areas of concentration, 119 respondents listed the colonial and revolutionary period, 57 the national period, 110 the middle period, 78 Civil War and Reconstruction, 113 the United States 1877–1900, 258 the United States 1900–1945, and 93 the United States since 1945. Eighteen did not specify a concentration. The largest subject-matter specialty represented was political history (175), followed by cultural and social history (133), diplomatic history (95), and intellectual history (61). The specialties listed by the fewest respondents were women's history (15), immigration and ethnic history (11), and history of the American Indian (11).[6]

No fewer than 98 different institutions were listed by the 846 respondents as having granted them Ph.D.'s. Of these, 26 institutions were named by 10 or more respondents, accounting for 70 percent of the total number. The largest group received the Ph.D. from the University of Wisconsin (70). Besides the University of Wisconsin, the institutions that granted doctorates to 25 or more respondents were Harvard University (49), University of California at Berkeley (41), Yale University (27), University of Virginia (27), University of Chicago (27), and the University of Illinois (25).[7] Of the total number of these 846 Ph.D.-holding historians, only 105 stated that they had published no articles or books since receiving the degree. Among the rest, the average number of articles produced was nine and the number of books authored, co-authored, or edited was three.[8]

As determined from the rankings supplied in Section IV of the survey, these historians judged four presidents to be Great—Lincoln, Franklin Roosevelt, Washington, and Jefferson. Four others were considered to be Near Great—Theodore Roosevelt, Wilson, Jackson, and Truman. Nine presidents were rated as Above Average—John Adams, Lyndon Johnson, Eisenhower, Polk, Kennedy, Madison, Monroe, John Quincy Adams, and Cleveland. Five presidents were rated as Failure—Andrew Johnson, Buchanan, Nixon, Grant, and Harding.[9]

These findings did not vary greatly from past polls, but there were some differences (see Table 1). In all previous polls Washington ranked second only to Lincoln. In the Murray-Blessing survey, Franklin Roosevelt moved up to second place, dropping Washington to third.[10] Although both Schlesinger polls had Wilson in the fourth slot, and the *Chicago Tribune* poll placed Theodore Roosevelt there, the Murray-Blessing historians put Jefferson in fourth place. The other high-ranked presidents also juggled their positions slightly. But whatever the minor variations from poll to poll, the three most recent ones agreed that the eight top-rated presidents were Lincoln, Washington, Franklin Roosevelt, Jefferson, Theodore Roosevelt, Wilson, Jackson, and Truman—with Lincoln, Washington, and Franklin Roosevelt being the consensus top three.

For the presidents occupying the middle categories, greater differences in the rankings appeared. Still, the names of the presidents in the middle groups, if not their rankings, generally remained the same. The most glaring differences occurred with Cleveland, John Quincy Adams, McKinley, and Eisenhower. The first Schlesinger poll ranked Cleveland eighth (Near Great). The second Schlesinger poll dropped him to eleventh. Then he fell to fifteenth in the Porter poll, rebounded to thirteenth in the *Chicago Tribune* poll, and plunged to seventeenth in the Murray-Blessing survey. John Quincy Adams, who began in the first Schlesinger poll as eleventh, fell in the second poll

TABLE 1. A Comparison of Polls

Murray-Blessing 1982 (N = 846)		Mode	Mean	Chicago Tribune 1982 (N = 49)	
Lincoln	Great	1	1.13	Lincoln	10 Best
F. Roosevelt		1	1.22	Washington	
Washington		1	1.27	F. Roosevelt	
Jefferson		1	1.70	T. Roosevelt	
T. Roosevelt	Near Great	2	1.93	Jefferson	
Wilson		2	2.07	Wilson	
Jackson		2	2.32	Jackson	
Truman		2	2.45	Truman	
J. Adams	Above Average	3	2.85	Eisenhower	
L. Johnson		3	2.87	Polk	
Eisenhower		3	2.99	McKinley	
Polk		3	3.06	L. Johnson	
Kennedy		3	3.13	Cleveland	
Madison		3	3.30	Kennedy	
Monroe		3	3.35	J. Adams ⎫ tie	
J. Q. Adams		3	3.42	Monroe ⎭	
Cleveland		3	3.43	Madison	
McKinley	Average	4	3.78	Van Buren	
Taft		4	3.87	J. Q. Adams	
Van Buren		4	3.97	Taft	
Hoover		4	4.03	Hoover	
Hayes		4	4.05	Hayes	
Arthur		4	4.24	Ford	
Ford		4	4.32	Arthur	
Carter		4	4.36	B. Harrison	
B. Harrison		4	4.40	Taylor	
Taylor	Below Average	5	4.45	Carter	
Tyler		5	4.61	Tyler	
Fillmore		5	4.64	Coolidge	
Coolidge		5	4.65	A. Johnson	10 Worst
Pierce		5	4.95	Fillmore	
A. Johnson	Failure	6	5.10	Grant	
Buchanan		6	5.15	Pierce	
Nixon		6	5.18	Buchanan	
Grant		6	5.25	Nixon	
Harding		6	5.56	Harding	

SOURCES: *Chicago Tribune Magazine*, Jan. 10, 1982, pp. 8–13, 15, 18; report on results of David L. Porter poll, 1981 (in Robert K. Murray's possession); *New York Times Magazine*, July 29, 1962, pp. 12–13, 40–41, 43; *Life*, Nov. 1, 1948, pp. 65–66, 68, 73–74.

TABLE 1 (cont'd)

	Porter 1981 (N = 41)	Schlesinger 1962 (N = 75)	Schlesinger 1948 (N = 55)
Great	Lincoln Washington F. Roosevelt Jefferson T. Roosevelt	Lincoln Washington F. Roosevelt Wilson Jefferson	Lincoln Washington F. Roosevelt Wilson Jefferson
Near Great	Wilson Jackson Truman Polk J. Adams L. Johnson	Jackson T. Roosevelt Polk Truman J. Adams Cleveland	Jackson T. Roosevelt Cleveland J. Adams Polk
Average	Eisenhower Madison Kennedy Cleveland McKinley Monroe J. Q. Adams Van Buren Hayes Taft Hoover Carter Arthur B. Harrison Ford	Madison J. Q. Adams Hayes McKinley Taft Van Buren Monroe Hoover B. Harrison Arthur Eisenhower A. Johnson	J. Q. Adams Monroe Hayes Madison Van Buren Taft Arthur McKinley A. Johnson Hoover B. Harrison
Below Average	Taylor Tyler Fillmore Coolidge A. Johnson Grant Pierce	Taylor Tyler Fillmore Coolidge Pierce Buchanan	Tyler Coolidge Fillmore Taylor Buchanan Pierce
Failure	Nixon Buchanan Harding	Grant Harding	Grant Harding

to thirteenth, and wound up in the last three surveys as eighteenth, nineteenth, and sixteenth. A different fate befell McKinley. He was eighteenth in the first Schlesinger survey, climbed in the second to fifteenth, fell one place in the Porter poll to sixteenth, rose to eleventh in the *Chicago Tribune* poll, and resumed the eighteenth position in the Murray-Blessing tabulation. Eisenhower made the most spectacular gain of any president in the middle categories. In the second Schlesinger poll he ranked a lowly twenty-second, jumped to twelfth in the Porter poll, rose to ninth in the *Chicago Tribune* poll, and came to rest as eleventh in the Murray-Blessing rankings.

As with the top-rated presidents, a much clearer consensus emerged in the cases of the lowest-rated ones. Historians might differ somewhat on the relative ranking of presidents in the middle categories, but they demonstrated no such doubt about who were the worst presidents in the nation's history. In every poll Harding remained firmly entrenched in last place. Either Grant or Buchanan appeared consistently in the next-to-last slot. Nixon was ranked either second or third from the bottom in the polls taken since his resignation. Pierce and Andrew Johnson were the two other presidents who repeatedly appeared in the lowest level.

The general similarity in these polls, especially the consistency of opinion about those at the top and bottom of the list, was immediately obvious. Yet the differences in the ranking of a few presidents, such as Eisenhower, made us wonder if similar rank changes could be expected for some other presidents in the future. To help determine this, we first figured out the relative "controversiality factor" for all of the presidents by plotting the deviation (or swing) in the respondents' rankings of each one. Expected and unexpected results appeared. The four most controversial presidents (that is, those receiving the widest distribution of ratings) were Nixon, Lyndon Johnson, Hoover, and Jackson. Of these four, Nixon was by far the most controversial. John Quincy Adams, Andrew Johnson, Truman, Wilson, Carter, Polk, and Kennedy were next in line after Jackson. Conversely, the three *least* controversial of *all* the presidents were Washington, Franklin Roosevelt, and Lincoln. These findings suggested that in future surveys the positions of Nixon, Lyndon Johnson, and Hoover were more likely to change than those of other presidents; in particular, the scatterplots of rankings versus the age of the historian suggest that Johnson will move down and Nixon will move up. Although Jackson was also in this top controversial group, it was difficult to believe that his ranking would actually change much in view of the general consistency with which historians have rated him in all the various polls. Besides Lyndon Johnson and Nixon, of the most recent presidents, Truman, Kennedy, and Carter apparently were more likely to have a change in rating than Eisenhower and Ford (probably downward for both Truman and Kennedy, again because of the distribution of their scatterplots). On the other hand, it seemed *very* unlikely that any shift would occur for Franklin Roosevelt (see Appendix 2).

After determining whether any significant rank changes could be expected on the basis of the controversiality factor, the next question was whether the personal, academic, and demographic data contained in Section I significantly influenced the respondents' ratings in Section IV. First, the ratings of the presidents by all respondents was compared with those by the various age groups within the survey sample to detect if there were any significant variations on this score. The basic finding was not too surprising: the older the respondent, the more lenient the judgment of presidential performances. Of the presidents who received *statistically* different ratings from the various age groups, Cleveland was rated more harshly by the younger historians than by the older ones. The same was true for Buchanan and Andrew Johnson. Hoover received his lowest rating from the youngest group of historians (those under forty) and was rated highest by those over sixty-five, who, ironically, were the children of the Great Depression. A natural question immediately arose: As the younger historians grow older, will they too become more lenient, or does this portend that Cleveland, Buchanan, Andrew Johnson, and Hoover will rise no higher than their current rankings, and even drop lower as the older historians die off? Wilson too may be destined to climb no higher in the rankings, since historians fifty-five years of age and over showed him much greater respect than did the younger groups. Truman, in particular, represented an intriguing case: the two older groups (age fifty-five and older) ranked him higher than did the middle group (age forty-five through fifty-four), and all these were much more sympathetic to him than the two youngest age groups (age forty-four and below). This would seem to foreshadow an inevitable drop for Truman. Conversely, no significant trends appeared in the different age-groups regarding the top three presidents—Lincoln, Franklin Roosevelt, and Washington—and no change can be foreseen for them on the basis of the respondents' age factor (see Appendix 3).[11]

Comparing ratings by the sex of the respondent offered a few additional insights. Disappointingly small, the female sample of fifty-nine still proved sufficient to establish several verifiable differences. Women historians in general were harsher in their assessment of presidential performances than men were. Washington and Polk, in particular, received severe treatment at their hands. Female ratings of these two presidents were almost half a category lower than the ratings by males (defining Great, Near Great, etc., as a full category). Four statistically significant exceptions to these lower ratings were evident, however. Grant, Kennedy, Lyndon Johnson, and Carter were all rated higher by women historians than by men. Is it conceivable that if substantially more women become historians the collective ratings of Washington and Polk would suffer and those of the other already-named presidents would benefit?[12] (See Appendix 4.)

At the outset of the study, we suspected that regional differences might affect historians' attitudes toward the presidents—hence the reason for asking respondents to state their place of birth and source of education. However, the results obtained by comparing the respondents' rankings by region of birth and by region of their Ph.D. degree-granting institution proved inconclusive. Only when the respondents' region of birth *and* region of the Ph.D.-granting institution were the same did any statistically significant variations appear—and then it involved only a few presidents. The North (meaning historians born in and receiving the Ph.D. in a northern state) rated Rutherford B. Hayes much higher than either the South or the Midwest. The South ranked Fillmore higher by as much as two-thirds of a category than any other regional group. The South was also much more tolerant of Buchanan and Andrew Johnson. On the other hand, the South was far harsher on Grant. The North, in turn, was much harder on Polk than was the South. The Midwest ranked Truman higher and the North rated him lower. The Midwest was also the most lenient on Eisenhower, while the South was the most severe (see Appendix 5).

Much better founded was our suspicion that historians working in the era of a particular president would tend to be more sympathetic toward him than would those specializing in another time period. In almost every instance this was true. A few cases were striking. John Quincy Adams was rated much higher by pre–Civil War historians than by those working in the periods after 1860. The same situation held for Fillmore and Taylor. Presidents less well known to the total sample benefited most from this tendency. Hayes, McKinley, and Taft, for example, were rated much higher by post–Civil War historians than by those concentrating their work in the pre–Civil War period. Only two statistically verifiable exceptions to this general rule appeared: Pierce and Andrew Johnson. Pierce was rated much higher by Civil War and post–Civil War historians than by pre–Civil War historians. On the other hand, Andrew Johnson was ranked much lower by Civil War and post–Civil War historians than by pre–Civil War historians.[13]

Subject-matter specialties played a different role in shading the presidential ratings. Generally speaking, it mattered not at all whether the respondent was a political, diplomatic, economic, intellectual, or social and cultural historian—there were no significant deviations in their rankings. But some intriguing exceptions occurred involving historians specializing in southern history, black history, military history, and women's history. Except for the military historians (who downgraded him severely), Carter was judged far more leniently by all these specialty groups than by the rest of the total sample. Southern and Afro-American historians were especially favorably disposed toward Carter. Fillmore and Polk were rated far higher by southern historians than by others, but this group was the harshest of all the specialists in ranking Grant and Eisenhower. On the other hand, military historians ranked Eisenhower significantly higher and Madison significantly lower than did any of the other groups. Afro-American historians rated Andrew Johnson and Polk lower than did historians in the other specialties. There was a full category's difference between Andrew Johnson's rating by Afro-American historians and his rating by the political historians. Interesting also was the wide divergence in Jefferson's rating between the Afro-American historians, who gave him his lowest rating, and historians of the West and the frontier, who gave him the highest. Women's history specialists rated Washington lower by as much as two-thirds of a category than did any of the others. They treated Polk and Theodore Roosevelt in much the same way. The only historians who rated the Rough Rider lower than women's history specialists were those concentrating their work in legal and constitutional history (see Appendix 6).[14]

In trying to determine what influence the respondent's publication record had on his or her rating of presidents, we were mildly surprised to discover no statistically significant difference between those who had published much, those who had published some, and those who had not published at all. Nonpublishing historians showed no greater variations for given presidents than historians who had published—nor did their overall rankings differ. This held true even when the most prolific publishers were compared with those who had not published. Hence, a random survey sample selected only from historians with many publications would have yielded no significantly different rankings than from either a random sample of the total population or from those who had published nothing.[15]

Nor did the source of the Ph.D. degree appear to have any influence on the final rankings outcome. There were only marginal and insignificant variations in the rankings by those who received their doctorates from less well known institutions and by those whose degrees came from the best-known and most prestigious universities. The same was true for the ratings by those who secured their Ph.D. from small graduate programs and by those from the largest programs. Because the "eastern historical establishment" had been charged with overrepresentation in past presidential polls, we also compared the ratings of historians having doctorates from "eastern" schools with those having doctorates from schools elsewhere, and again found so little variation as to be insignificant. [16]

In retrospect, the Murray-Blessing survey, both because of its sample size and its inclusion of personal and academic respondent data, added considerably to our knowledge about the human factors influencing presidential ratings. Still, this survey can be criticized because it contained shortcomings that were evident to its authors from the beginning. The limited scope and time constraints of the survey instrument prevented an analysis of the historical literature on the presidents and its influence on the historians' rankings. How many of the respondents were *actually* conversant with the latest historical writings on the presidents, or had read the most significant and scholarly presidential biographies, was something we did not know. Further, this study had no way within its brief compass to determine precisely *what* historical literature the respondents had been exposed to concerning each president and whether that exposure had affected their rankings. More famous or popular presidents may have commanded more scholarly interest from the respondents during their academic careers and therefore received more attention from them in the rankings. Moreover, historical researchers and biographers who knew the lives of *individual* presidents best were inevitably submerged in the rest of the survey population, and their expert judgment was lost in the mass of general statistics. The survey was simply not designed to compare or contrast the presidential ranking results of the many with these few. Readers who want to do that can select from among the many extant presidential biographies and also consult Bailey's *Presidential Greatness*. Although it is conjecture on our part, these particular respondents, especially those specializing in the lesser-known chief executives, probably believe that their own presidents should rank higher than the collective ratings showed. However, as indicated earlier, the *Chicago Tribune* poll of 1982 used such "expert" respondents exclusively without many significant differences surfacing.

Similarly, it was beyond the limited scope of this study to discover the actual *depth* of knowledge of the individual respondents about the individual presidents involved. Dividing the survey into three separate time periods and requesting that only those specializing in that period answer the questions was at best a modest attempt on our part to get at this problem. There was no framework in the study to determine whether a lack of knowledge about the presidents caused respondents simply to follow the line of least resistance and merely indicate in their rankings what they already intuitively knew—that certain presidents have traditionally been regarded by historians as being more successful than others. Finally, this survey had no specific provision for gauging the precise impact on presidential rankings that the recent changes in the historical profession have caused or are causing. Our attempt to discover the thinking of those in certain subject-matter specialties within the profession was at best only marginally successful in attacking this problem. For some time, political history has been losing favor among historians as a research field, and the profession as a whole may have even less specific information as more of its members move into other areas of specialization, such as women's history, black history, and so on.

All these matters require additional study, and as research skills in quantification increase perhaps other surveys will come along to fill in the gaps. In the meantime, the findings of the Murray-Blessing survey support a number of important conclusions. First, of the total variation in any given president's *collective* rating, only a small part of it—somewhat less than 15 percent—could be traced statistically to demographic and academic characteristics associated with the responding historians. Using all the data and every test available, the Murray-Blessing survey was unable to connect any ranking of a president primarily to any single demographic or academic factor or combination of factors (see Appendix 7).[17] In a few instances, demographic and academic considerations affected individual or group responses, but they did not *significantly* change the total sample's collective response.[18]

Second, there were strong indications that future surveys would not change these rankings much. Although certain presidents in the middle categories might move slightly up or down, the ones who appeared at the top and bottom of the list would probably remain there (only Truman and Nixon might prove to be exceptions). Indeed, the general consistency with which professional historians have rated all the presidents since the first Schlesinger poll in 1948 suggests that the rankings of most of the past presidents are, within relatively narrow limits, rather firmly fixed.

Finally, this survey, like the others, could not provide an answer to why one president was ranked eighteenth and another nineteenth, or one seventeenth and another twentieth. Such fine distinctions were more an accident of statistical accounting than of discriminating judgment on the part of the historians. Also, despite the general agreement among the polls on the presidents in the major categories, the exact lines between Average and Above Average or Average and Below Average were difficult to draw and even when drawn possessed only limited meaning. However, the remarkable consensus among all these historians on the presidents *at the top* and *at the bottom* of the performance ladder did suggest that they had in mind more than vague and uncritical generalities when they evaluated presidential performances. It was this agreement, along with the historians' answers to the questions in Sections II and III of the survey instrument (which are reproduced in Appendix 1), that provided the basis for the analyses that follow and that justified the attempt to determine the ingredients of what constitutes greatness in the White House. It also supplies the main reason why analyzing historians' thinking on the presidency is worthy of study.

THREE

Do Appearance and Background Affect Presidential Success?

IN THE EARLY DAYS OF THE REPUBLIC, few Americans ever saw their president, and until the advent of movie news in the early twentieth century, most could describe their president only on the basis of official photographs or newspaper pictures. But in the recent period, because of almost unlimited television exposure, his face has become as familiar as faces in our own family. As a result, the president's physical appearance has acquired increasing importance, especially in the eyes of the media and the general public. Certainly how he looks has become a much talked-about factor in successfully seeking the presidency. But has this attribute really contributed to the success of presidents or to how historians have rated their performance once they were in the White House?

As a group, the presidents varied in their physical attributes. Most of them, however, were quite average. A few were thought to be "handsome." Kennedy might have been a movie star. Reagan was one. Fillmore was considered to be exceedingly "good-looking," and in 1920 Harding captured the votes of hundreds of thousands of newly enfranchised women partly because he "looked like a president." On the other hand, John Quincy Adams and Martin Van Buren were decidedly unimposing, and Lincoln, the butt of many jokes about his appearance, frequently commented about his homeliness himself. Presidents have also come in all shapes and sizes. Madison was the shortest at 5'4". He was also the smallest president, weighing little more than 100 pounds. Taft was the largest, tipping the scales at over 320. Lincoln was the tallest chief executive, soaring to 6'4½". Presidents, as a group, have been taller than the average height for the adult male population;

indeed, sixteen, including such recent ones as Franklin Roosevelt, Lyndon Johnson, Kennedy, Ford, and Reagan, have stood six feet or more.

Such facts may be interesting, but any connection with presidential success in the Murray-Blessing survey was nonexistent.[1] A pleasing physical appearance may indeed be important to a successful presidential candidacy in the modern media age, but it had no bearing at all on the historians' assessments of presidential performances of the past. When asked, 75 percent flatly disagreed that presidential "looks" contributed as much to his success as his abilities. The survey historians were of like mind on this point, regardless of the time period of their research or teaching concentration.[2] Among the eight factors considered potentially significant for presidential success in the pre-Civil War era (integrity, intelligence, charisma, patriotism, sensitivity to popular demands, previous political experience, an aristocratic bearing, and a pleasing physical appearance), historians rated a pleasing physical appearance at the bottom and an aristocratic bearing just above it. For the modern period since 1945, they elevated a pleasing physical appearance two notches to sixth place, indicating that constant media exposure may be having some impact on contemporary historical assessments (see Appendix 8).[3] Our attempts, however, to prove or disprove this possibility were mixed. Recalling the Nixon five-o'clock shadow and posters asking "Would You Buy a Used Car from This Man?" we asked the respondents to rank the importance of the following seven factors in contributing to Nixon's downfall: animus of the media, his apparent duplicity, his use of presidential power, his Vietnam actions, his physical image, his economic policies, and the "eastern" establishment. The historians ranked Nixon's physical image second to last, far below his apparent duplicity and his use of presidential power, their number-one and number-two choices. Still, only 35 percent of the respondents were willing to state categorically that Nixon's physical appearance had no significance whatever in his failure as president.[4]

Leisure-time habits of the presidents also failed to correlate in any way with the historians' rankings. This came as no surprise, even though some presidents were roundly criticized in their day for certain of their off-hour pursuits, such as gambling, drinking, and smoking. Of more interest is the fact that there was also no correlation between the rankings of the presidents and their work habits. The hardest-working presidents were not viewed by the historians as the most successful. Carter was a case in point, and so was Harding—both men often working late into the night.

Even a brief glance at the rankings indicates that the age of a president also made very little difference to his historical standing. (See Appendix 9 for pertinent data on presidential backgrounds.) The ages of the three top-rated presidents upon taking office were 52 (Lincoln), 57 (Washington), and 51 (Franklin Roosevelt). Those of the bottom three were 55 (Harding), 46 (Grant), and 56 (Nixon). The youngest presidents were Theodore Roosevelt (42), Kennedy (43), Grant (46), Cleveland (47), Pierce (48), and Garfield (49). The rankings of these presidents ranged from fifth (Theodore Roosevelt, Near Great) to the thirty-fifth (Grant, Failure). The oldest Presidents (excluding Reagan, who was almost 70 when he was inaugurated) were W. H. Harrison (68), Buchanan (65), Taylor (64), Eisenhower (62), John Adams (61), Jackson (61), Ford (61), and Truman (60). Their rankings spread from seventh (Jackson, Near Great) to thirty-third (Buchanan, Failure).

Beyond these facts, which disclosed no significance in the age factor, one interesting pattern did emerge. On a scale of 1 to 6, with 1 representing "Great" and over 5 "Failure," the average ranking for presidents in their forties—Theodore Roosevelt, Kennedy, Grant, Cleveland, and Pierce (Garfield was not ranked)—was 3.73. For those in their sixties—Truman, Ford, Jackson, John Adams, Eisenhower, Taylor, and Buchanan (Harrison was not ranked)—was 3.61. For presidents in their fifties, the average was 3.54. We were somewhat surprised that the youngest group of presidents should come off statistically the worst.

Rarely has age been a campaign issue in presidential politics, although both age and health have had an impact on presidential history. With life expectancy increasing and the population growing older, we can probably expect to see older candidates running for the office, and therefore presidents who are older than presidents have been before. Still, the tasks of the presidency are admittedly more suited to the young than to the old. William H. Harrison, the oldest president until Reagan, caught pneumonia on inauguration day and died thirty-two days later. Zachary Taylor, the third-oldest president, died one year and 127 days after entering the White House. Eisenhower, the fourth-oldest president, was hospitalized three times, suffering a heart attack and undergoing major abdominal surgery. Reagan's various medical problems are well known. In assessing the toll the presidency takes on the health of the incumbent, one is confronted by the early deaths of such presidents as Polk (53), Arthur (56), Theodore Roosevelt (60), Coolidge (60), and Harding (57). On the other hand, many of the early presidents, as well as some later ones, were especially long-lived—John Adams (90), John Q. Adams (80), Jefferson (83), Madison (85), Hoover (90), and Truman (88).

Until recently, the chief executive's health was a matter between himself and his physician. For example, the nation did not know about Jackson's many infirmities; Cleveland's operation for cancer of the jaw was kept secret; Wilson's precise condition following his stroke was walled within the White House; Harding's heart trouble was not a topic for public conversation; and Franklin Roosevelt's exact condition at the time of Yalta was withheld from public knowledge. However, with the coming of Eisenhower, details concerning the president's health became public property. Will health matters henceforth play a larger role in presidential assessments? Professor Clinton Rossiter has claimed that health, "in the sense of exemption from ailments," is necessary to a person in the presidential office. Perhaps so. But if we can believe the rankings in the Murray-Blessing survey, this was not true in the past. Of the eight presidents rated as Great or Near Great, five suffered ill health while in the White House.[5]

Not only did the historians' rankings show that age and health played no part in their decisions, but their answers to the survey's questions underscored it. Only 37 percent felt that the constitutionally endorsed age of thirty-five was too young to be president. Similarly, 72 percent overwhelmingly rejected the notion that a person of seventy was too old to be president. When asked the question directly, 68 percent agreed that presidential age had little or no significance in relation to presidential success. Significantly, the ages of the responding historians themselves showed no variation in their answers to these age-related queries.[6]

Religion too had no impact on the historians' rankings of the presidents, although religion, more than age, has been an issue (sometimes an unspoken one) in presidential elections. While in the White House, most presidents wore their religion lightly (Carter being the most recent exception). Even if they were devout church members before becoming president, they generally downplayed it. Most of them attended nonsectarian church services while in office, or moved around from one church to another, considering any partisan display of religion too risky.

None of the presidents that the historians rated as Great was noted for his religiosity. Lincoln, although a believer in God, had no church attachment, and Jefferson, a Deist, was attacked by some contemporaries as being a radical freethinker. Conversely, religiosity had no influence either positively or negatively in the historians' assessments of such presidents as McKinley, Hoover, and Carter, men deeply committed to their particular faiths.[7]

Although it played no role in their ratings, the Murray-Blessing historians did believe religion could have a *potentially* dangerous influence on presidential performance. The tendency of recent administrations and presidential candidates to inject religion into the political arena has unquestionably fanned this belief. The historians were firm in their opinion on several points. More than 61 percent disagreed that a person possessing a deep religious faith was preferable to an atheist or an agnostic in the White House. Only 13 percent believed that a deeply committed believer would make a better president than one who was not so deeply committed. A majority of the historians participating in the face-to-face interviews felt keenly that the deeper (or more "emotionally held") the religious commitment, the greater the danger to a president's success. Similarly, 64 percent of the mail survey historians stated that a president should not allow his religious beliefs to dictate his political decisions.[8]

As one might have expected, birth and ancestry also figured little in the actual rankings of past presidents. Most of the presidents were born in rural or small-town environments. Only Theodore Roosevelt (born in New York City), Taft (in Cincinnati, Ohio), Kennedy (in Brookline, Massachusetts), and Ford (in Omaha, Nebraska) could be considered exceptions. Historians did not consider this matter significant in relation to presidential performance. When asked in the survey whether an urban or a rural and small-town background was preferable, even in a modern president, the responding historians split down the middle (48 percent agreed; 52 percent disagreed), indicating they did not feel strongly one way or the other.[9] Moreover, a president's state of birth and region of political origin were likewise treated by the historians as having no special meaning. There were historic, political, and demographic reasons why so many presidents have come from the states of Virginia (8), Ohio (7), and New York (4)—a pattern that is already changing, since of the last eleven presidents (through Bush) only four were born east of the Mississippi. But none of these reasons related in any way to presidential competence or success in the White House.

As for presidential ancestry: seventeen presidents came from predominantly English stock; seven were Scotch-Irish; five were a combination of English and Scotch-Irish; two were Scotch (Monroe and Hayes); and two were Irish (Kennedy and Reagan). Thus, no less than thirty-three of the thirty-nine presidents (including W. H. Harrison, Garfield, and Reagan) possessed English, Scotch, or Irish blood. Exceptions to this near-monopoly were the two Roosevelts and Van Buren, who were Dutch; Jefferson, who was Welsh; and Hoover and Eisenhower, who were Swiss-German. With so few variations among presidential bloodlines to consider, it is not surprising that the historians simply ignored it.

The marital status of a president, like birth and ancestry, also had no impact on the historians' rankings. Some presidents, such as Lincoln and

McKinley, were afflicted while in office by difficult or ill wives who added immeasurably to their burdens. Others, like Hoover and Kennedy, were aided by their wives' grace and charm. But only rarely did a president rely on his wife for information or political advice, as Franklin Roosevelt did with Eleanor. And only once did a president's wife actually intrude on the affairs of state, as the second Mrs. Wilson did during her husband's illness. Most presidents' wives remained discreetly in the background, prompting public attention only intermittently.

Even though a First Lady knew the president better than anyone else, and her actions could admittedly affect her husband's mood and thinking, that chemistry was ignored by the historians in the ranking process. When asked directly, however, they expressed a belief that the First Lady *could* be a positive influence in a presidential administration and *could* have a beneficial effect on her husband's overall reputation. Further, they condoned a First Lady playing more than a passive role in the White House and supported this view by using as an example Dolley Madison—a First Lady who compensated to a considerable extent for her husband's singular lack of personal charm. [10]

Not all the presidents had wives or were married while in office. Buchanan, the only president from Pennsylvania, was a bachelor and never married. Several presidents were married twice, six married widows, and four (counting Reagan) married divorcées. No president has married three times. Five presidents were without wives when they served, their spouses having died before they entered office. The number of children of presidents ranged from none for such presidents as Washington, Jackson, and Harding, to fifteen for John Tyler.

The point scarcely needs to be made: married, unmarried, more-than-once married, childless, or widowed—the historical rankings of the presidents revealed absolutely no connection with any of these personal factors. Yet the Murray-Blessing historians did show some bias in their thinking when asked certain marriage-related questions. A very large minority (43 percent) believed that marriage *was* important and preferred to have a person in the White House who was married to one who was not. The older the historian, the more likely they were to be in this sizable minority. Even more interesting was the attitude of the survey respondents about how many divorces were acceptable for a president. Only a bare majority (54 percent) countenanced one divorce, and only 21 percent found as many as three acceptable. (Reagan was the nation's only divorced president.) Again, the older historians were more conservative than the younger historians in their responses. [11]

The educational background of the presidents was a factor that Ph.D.-holding historians might have been expected to elevate to considerable importance in the rating process, yet an examination of the relationship between presidential educational backgrounds and the rankings leaves doubt on this score. Nine of the presidents had no education beyond grammar or high school, and four of these men (Taylor, Fillmore, Lincoln, and Andrew Johnson) had no formal education at all. Lincoln, rated by the historians as the premier president, was largely self-taught, and Jackson, judged as Near Great, had only a rudimentary education.

Most presidents, however, had earned a college degree of some sort. Of the first six presidents, only Washington did not have one. Of the nation's twentieth-century presidents, only two did not possess a four-year college degree. Truman, ranked as Near Great, did not attend college at all, and Harding, the bottom-ranked president, completed only a two-year course at the now-defunct Ohio Central College. Altogether, the presidents received their degrees from twenty-one different institutions. Excluding the three presidents who attended the service academies—Eisenhower and Grant (West Point) and Carter (Annapolis)—only three of the presidents attended a public or state-supported school: Polk (North Carolina), Lyndon Johnson (Southwestern Texas State College), and Ford (Michigan). All others had a private-school education. Harvard University headed the list with five presidents. Next came William and Mary College with three and Princeton with two.

On an individual-to-individual basis, no pattern regarding academic backgrounds and the historians' ratings emerged. A college degree obviously did not ensure presidential success, nor did the absence of one preclude it. A random group of presidents who did not graduate from college could include such chief executives as Lincoln (first), Washington (third), Jackson (seventh), and Truman (eighth). On the other hand, it might also include Van Buren (twentieth), Taylor (twenty-seventh), Fillmore (twenty-ninth), and Andrew Johnson (thirty-second). Those who had four-year college degrees, in turn, were ranked all the way from Franklin Roosevelt (second) to Grant (thirty-fifth). Nor was there any significance found in the source of a presidential education. The single possible exception was Harvard, which produced more presidents than any other school, a success rate that is noteworthy. The combined rating (2.51) of the two Roosevelts, Kennedy, and the two Adamses placed this Harvard group of five presidents on the line between the Above Average and Near Great categories.

One other possibly significant education-related combination emerged. When the presidents were grouped into historical eras, the following lineup occurred:[12]

Presidents	Historical Era and No. in Category	Combined Rankings	Presidents w/o 4-year Degrees
Washington—J. Q. Adams	1789–1829 (6)	2.64	1
F. Roosevelt–Carter	1933–1981 (8)	3.31	1
T. Roosevelt—Hoover	1901–1933 (6)	3.68	1
Lincoln—McKinley	1861–1901 (10)	3.92	4
Jackson—Buchanan	1829–1861 (9)	4.14	5

Is this more than coincidence? It would seem from this listing that the possession of a college degree by presidents, if not individually significant, may have had a collective importance over a given period of time. But perhaps not. It could be argued that in the top two historical eras in the rankings shown above, the one noncollege president in each (Washington and Truman) actually helped rather than hurt that group's standing.

Although more than seven out of ten of the survey historians agreed that education was not a *reliable* indicator of presidential performance, they were extremely forthright about what they considered to be the "proper" educational background for a contemporary president. More than 60 percent believed that the president should have at least a four-year college degree.[13] Moreover, these historians agreed that the college training of future presidents should concentrate more in the humanities and social sciences than in the natural or physical sciences. The historians undoubtedly displayed a bit of academic chauvinism here, but they based their belief on the assumption that the presidency will remain essentially a humanistically oriented office, even though the nation might live in an increasingly technological world. Again probably betraying some bias, the respondents ranked (in order of importance) the disciplines in which a contemporary president should have considerable knowledge as follows: American history, economics, other cultures, and political science. Below these, and in order, came: international law, natural or physical science, and military science.[14] Where this education should be secured was of no great concern to the majority of the historians. Some 67 percent claimed that although most of the presidents were educated in private institutions, individuals trained there were no better prepared for the presidency than those educated in publicly supported institutions.[15]

While somewhat ambivalent about the impact the educational background of a president had on his ultimate success, the historians considered his political and occupational background experience to be a more serious matter. In general, they agreed with Columbia University history Professor Richard Hofstadter, who once asserted that the best career qualification for a president was "to be a professional politician of long standing, preferably (though not necessarily) in both legislative and executive experience."[16] At first glance, the historical record would seem to agree. Before Zachary Taylor, all presidents had served either in Congress or in the Continental Congress. Taking the thirty-nine presidents together (including W. H. Harrison, Garfield, and Reagan), sixteen were former senators, eighteen were representatives, and eleven served in both houses. Fifteen were governors, thirteen were vice-presidents, six were secretaries of state (mainly the early presidents), three were secretaries of war (Monroe, Grant, and Taft), and one was secretary of commerce (Hoover). On the other hand, eleven presidents never had any real political responsibilities before becoming chief executive, and several others had only very limited national political experience. Lincoln, for example, aside from his dabbling in local Illinois politics, served only a two-year term in the House of Representatives before entering the White House.

Clearly, there is some difficulty here. What the historians claimed and how they rated the individual presidents were often at variance on this matter. Actually, except for the early ones, few of the presidents had exposure to the full range of American political experience before entering the White House. Tyler served in local Virginia state politics, was U.S. representative, U.S. senator, governor, and finally was elected vice-president before assuming the presidency following W. H. Harrison's death. Buchanan spent thirty-nine years in public service, serving in the Pennsylvania state legislature, the U.S. House and Senate, as minister to Russia and to Great Britain, and as secretary of state. Coolidge ran for office twenty times, holding such positions as city councilman, mayor, Massachusetts state representative, state senator, lieutenant governor, governor, and vice-president. Andrew Johnson, like Coolidge, held virtually every elected position, from village alderman in his local community in Tennessee through vice-president of the United States. Yet all of these presidents—Tyler, Buchanan, Coolidge, and Andrew Johnson—were rated low, and two of them were designated failures.

Besides being vice-president or the governor of a large state, being a U.S. senator has historically provided the inside track to the White House. Since Franklin Roosevelt's day (to 1992), the two major parties have nominated for the presidency one general, six governors, six incumbent or former vice-presidents, and eight former or incumbent senators.

If the vice-presidency, the senate, or a governorship has been the preferred political route, the law has been the preferred profession from which to mount an assault on the White House. Twenty-four of the thirty-nine presidents were lawyers or had read for the bar. The second most common occupation has been the military—ten presidents were generals, although only four of them were "professional" military men (W. H. Harrison, Taylor, Grant, and Eisenhower). A number of the early presidents were plantation owners, but since the Civil War only two have been directly connected with agriculture—Lyndon Johnson and Carter. One president was an engineer (Hoover), one a journalist (Harding), one an educator (Wilson), and one an actor (Reagan). Six have described themselves as having no profession other than politics—Andrew Johnson, Cleveland, Theodore Roosevelt, Franklin Roosevelt, Truman, and Kennedy.

In ranking various political offices as the best training ground for the presidency, the historians agreed with the historical record by listing the U.S. Senate as number one. Following senator came governor and vice-president. Farther down the list they placed congressman, and much farther down, cabinet official and military officer.[17]

In ranking occupations and their training potential for the presidency, the historians supplied a few surprises. Among the various choices the survey offered, lawyer, as expected, was ranked by itself at the top. But then came, in order, corporate executive, journalist, and union leader. Bringing up the rear were banker, engineer, doctor, and church leader.[18] Although not given "educator" as a choice to select from among the professions, the historians were asked in a separate question whether they believed an academician constituted a poor presidential risk. Considering that they, themselves, were academicians and that Wilson, the lone educator-president, was judged by them to be Near Great, a remarkably high 36 percent declared that such a person *would* represent a presidential risk.[19]

Apparently these historians were saying that a lawyer and/or professional politician with experience as vice-president, senator, or governor represented the best presidential bet, but their rankings supported this premise only in part. The presidents who described themselves as professional politicians (Andrew Johnson, Cleveland, the two Roosevelts, Truman, and Kennedy) did come off best, having a combined rating of 2.87 (Above Average), despite Andrew Johnson's lowly position. Generals, whom the historians listed as among the poorest presidential possibilities, were next, with a combined rating of 3.71 (Average).[20] At the bottom were the presidents whom the historical record showed to have the *most* prepresidential political experience (Tyler, Buchanan, Andrew Johnson, and Coolidge), having a combined rating of only 4.87 (Below Average).

These ratings leave unanswered a number of questions, signaling that in the end the historians were influenced much more by other factors than by the previous occupational and political experience of the presidents being rated. Obviously, holding political office before running for president did not always benefit the individuals involved. As one recent study has shown, succession to the presidency through the vice-presidency has sometimes had a "negative impact" that was more apt to harm than help the person's effectiveness as president.[21] A number of observers, including some vice-presidents, have claimed that the vice-presidency was really worth nothing at all. Except for succession to the presidency through the unexpected death of an incumbent, the vice-presidency has been a dubious way to gain and hold on to the top spot.[22] Similarly, the Senate as a training ground for the presidency has left something to be desired. Unlike a president, senators can be absent much of the time from their jobs and can curry media exposure without bearing the consequences for their words or deeds. Moreover, the historical record shows that presidents who have had congressional experience have not necessarily been able to get more bills through Congress or to work better with that body (Truman, Kennedy, and Bush being the most recent examples). Likewise, a governorship, while it provided needed executive experience, remained basically a "local" job without any real national dimension and provided no foreign policy experience.

The survey historians evidently considered previous political experience in this broader setting and sometimes downgraded its importance in contributing to a successful presidential performance. Asked to choose among eight factors (intelligence, integrity, charisma, intense patriotism, aristocratic bearing, pleasing physical appearance, sensitivity to popular demands, and previous political experience) contributing to presidential success in the pre–Civil War era, the responding historians listed previous political experience only as number three. A similar result occurred for the period from 1865 to 1945. When asked to evaluate these eight criteria for the years since 1945, they dropped previous political experience to number five (see Appendix 8).[23]

This quixotic attitude toward occupational and political experience was also underscored by the way the historians answered certain questions about specific presidents. Asked whether they considered Madison to have had adequate training and experience to be a successful president, 95 percent unsurprisingly said yes. The same percentage claimed similarly for Lyndon Johnson. However, when asked the same question about Andrew Johnson and Coolidge (both of whom also had extensive previous political experience),

73 percent said no in the case of Andrew Johnson and 63 percent said no in the case of Coolidge. Conversely, although Truman had no college degree, had been a failure in business, and had little executive experience before assuming the presidency, 60 percent declared him to have been adequately prepared on both educational and political grounds. Equally interesting is that 71 percent of the respondents claimed Eisenhower's military experience was a valuable asset to his presidency, even though they ranked the military at the bottom of the occupational choices offered by the survey as providing proper training for the presidency.[24]

In some cases the historians were obviously guilty of reading history "backwards" when considering occupational and political experience and their relationship to presidential success. If the survey historians judged a president to have been successful on other grounds, they were inclined to claim that his background training was also adequate or good. The reverse was also true: If they judged a president Below Average or a Failure, they were apt to find defects in his previous occupational or political experience. In short, although the historians would probably be loath to admit it, they proved by their rankings as well as by their answers to the survey's questions what Merle Miller contended after completing his oral biographies of Truman and Lyndon Johnson: that you cannot tell much about a presidential performance from the background of a person before his actually holding the office. As Lyndon Johnson plaintively commented to Bill Moyers on the morning of his first day in the presidency: "You know, Bill, I've been in both the House and Senate and in all that time no one told me how to be President."[25]

FOUR

Character and Personality as Rating Criteria

HISTORIANS HAVE FREQUENTLY made qualitative statements about the nature of presidential success on the basis of past presidential polls even though no concrete data was offered to support them. Following his 1948 survey, Professor Schlesinger claimed his results showed that great presidents were strong moral leaders of sound character, were expanders of executive power, and were connected with some turning point in the nation's history. Commenting on the United States Historical Society poll of 1977, Professor Henry S. Commager stated that American historians saw great presidents as being intelligent, having integrity of character, and being on "the side of the people" (defined by Commager as always pushing for progress through reform). [1]

In almost all such statements, presidential personality and character occupied a central theme. In attempting to validate such assumptions, the Murray-Blessing survey ran into numerous problems, discovering that although the connection between personality, character, and presidential success was indeed important, it was also very difficult to delineate.

Presidential personalities have varied widely. Jackson was impulsive and autocratic; Benjamin Harrison rarely showed any emotion and was referred to as a "human iceberg"; Coolidge possessed a vindictive streak and wore a vinegar countenance; Franklin Roosevelt was often devious while exuding great charm; Eisenhower frequently displayed a violent temper; and Lyndon Johnson was a whole bundle of contradictions—cruel and kind, generous and greedy, crafty and naive. In short, every president presented a different and unique face to the public.

Complicating any assessment of the linkage between personality traits and presidential success was the fact that many such traits were double-edged. For example, loyalty to friends, potentially a "good" quality, was seen by the historians as crippling in the case of Harding and Grant, but in the case of Truman this "defect" was largely excused. Eisenhower's charm and sociability were considered to be winning attributes contributing to the success of his administration, yet the absence of them was not viewed as damaging to the standing of Wilson. So it went with all the presidents. In assigning the label "good" or "bad" to personality traits, the survey historians were flexible and situation-oriented. Generally, they isolated specific events of an administration that were affected by certain of the president's personality traits and then judged those traits to be either good or bad depending upon the successful or unsuccessful outcome of those situations.

In this regard, the president's *personal* morals, as opposed to his *public* morals, were treated leniently by the historians. On minor matters, such as profanity, they showed no concern whatsoever. Even on such a touchy subject as marital infidelity, only a bare majority (51 percent) said they would downgrade a president for it. The low rating they gave Harding, for example, was not crucially dependent on his alleged sexual escapades, nor did such a factor apparently color the historians' thinking on other presidents, such as Cleveland, Kennedy, or Franklin Roosevelt—all of whom had skeletons in their closets.[2]

Whatever the specific manifestations of his personal morality or his other personality traits, the overall impact of a successful president's total image was expected to be extraordinary. The most frequent word used by the interviewed historians to describe this impact was "charismatic." The mail survey historians also utilized this term. They invariably ranked high the presidents who they agreed were charismatic; those who were not thought to have charisma were ranked lower. In no case did they consider that any of the Below Average or Failure presidents had charisma. Conversely, they declared that all the top-ranked presidents were charismatic to some degree. Considering the differences in personalities among the Great and Near Great presidents, this conclusion seemed strange. If third-ranked Washington and sixth-ranked Wilson, with their austere and aloof manners, were judged to be charismatic, it was certainly a different kind of charisma than Franklin Roosevelt's (who was ranked second) or Eisenhower's (who was ranked eleventh). And Harding (the bottom-ranked president) actually possessed a winning personality that if it did not appeal to the survey historians, caused him to be regarded as charismatic by the press and electorate of his day.

The historians saved themselves, perhaps, by seeing charisma as only the most visible and not the most significant personality trait contributing to presidential success.[3] When considering each of the major time periods in American history (to 1865, 1865 to 1945, and since 1945), the historians ranked charisma in a president no higher than third in importance among eight factors. It is noteworthy, however, that charisma (which the interviewed historians also constantly connected with "image" and "style") gained in importance as one moved into the modern period. Ranked behind intelligence, integrity, previous political experience, sensitivity to popular demands, and patriotism in the period before 1865, charisma was named ahead of all others, except for intelligence and integrity, in the period since 1945 (see Appendix 8).[4]

All respondents agreed that intelligence and integrity were two of the most important personality traits linked with a successful presidential performance. They ranked intelligence high on the list of desirable qualities for a president in every time period (see Appendix 8).[5] Intelligence, as distinct from educational training or academic achievement, was admittedly difficult to assess, yet the historians were convinced that they recognized it when it was present. Its manifestations included not only mental agility and sharpness but also a capacity for growth and the constant use of "common sense." Not surprisingly, the historians considered the top-rated presidents to have "intelligence," and judged the lower-rated ones to have less of it.

The did not contend, however, that every president who had a good intellect made a good president. They saw intelligence and intellect as being two different things. Carter, who was sixtieth out of 820 in his Annapolis class, was assumed to possess a good intellect but he was given a low Average ranking. Similarly, Nixon, who was rated a Failure, was not downgraded because of a lack of brain power. Both Nixon and Carter were found wanting on other grounds. Kennedy's rating, on the other hand, definitely benefited from the historians' belief that his ability to learn quickly rested on an underlying intelligence. Truman also was helped by the historians' conviction that a sound intelligence provided him with a tremendous capacity for growth. The Murray-Blessing historians obviously regarded the Executive Mansion as a politician's institute for advanced learning that could house an unfinished man if he had the ability to develop. Ford's ranking, unfortunately, apparently suffered from the historians' perception, right or wrong, that he did not have this ability to grow in the office.[6]

Along with intelligence, integrity was consistently selected by the historians as a crucial trait. In the interviews the word "integrity" was frequently interchanged with the term "character." Some interviewees linked the two words together—integrity of character. In either case, both integrity and character were used to embrace a whole family of other highly prized qualities, such as sincerity, honesty, high ethical standards, sound principles, and self-discipline. Like intelligence, this set of virtues was often difficult to spot amid the dross of day-to-day political activities. Yet the historians, both in the mail survey and in the interviews, claimed that they found integrity or character present in *every* successful president.

In viewing the individual presidents, the historians applied this "character" yardstick rigidly. On Truman, for example, they agreed with Eric Sevareid, who once said of the Missourian, "Chance, in good part, took [him] to the presidency, but it was his character that kept him there and determined his historical fate."[7] They used a contrast between Eisenhower and Nixon to underscore the same point. Character, they declared, was one of Eisenhower's strongest qualities, a whopping 95 percent claiming it was an asset in his presidential ranking. Conversely, a near-unanimous 98 percent viewed Nixon's duplicity (i.e., lack of character) as being significant in his political failure.[8]

Although character was considered by the survey historians to be very important in influencing their presidential ratings, some of the associated qualities the term embraced were subject to certain interesting caveats. Historians, like the general public, wanted their presidents to be honest, 63 percent stating that honesty was always the best policy for the chief executive. But 72 percent also admitted that to be effective a president had to possess some cunning and at times be less than frank.[9] Cunning is not a trait that is usually admired. Still, the historians believed that a degree of it was desirable in a president so that he could manipulate people and events more skillfully. Further, a majority of the mail survey historians stated that they would permit a president to give out misleading information in certain restricted situations (e.g., to protect national security)—hardly a prescription for complete honesty. They also indicated that too rigid a public morality in a president was confining and that he should be allowed flexibility in choosing not only ends but also means.[10]

The rankings confirmed these subtleties. Lincoln, the premier president, was one of the most flexible chief executives in history, exhibiting a careful balance between determination and adaptability. Franklin Roosevelt, whom the historians ranked second, was another of the nation's most flexible politicians.[11] FDR's mastery of the art of crafty political maneuvering still causes many historical arguments, but this has not adversely affected his ranking. Similarly, Lyndon Johnson was often less than honest with the American people yet was rated number ten. On the other hand, Rutherford Hayes, who possessed no guile and ran his administration with such rectitude that he was sometimes called "His Honesty," was consigned by these same historians to only twenty-second place.

The *single* most critical personality trait for the historians was neither intelligence nor character, but one more closely linked with actual presidential performance—decisiveness. This trait, even when not articulated by the historians, remained at the center of their thinking when most connections were made between presidential personalities and presidential actions. Often the relationship between intelligence or character and presidential actions was difficult to define. But this was not the case with decisiveness. One statistical analysis of the Schlesinger polls of 1948 and 1962 discovered that general presidential prestige was broadly related to presidential "activeness," with decision-making playing a key role.[12] Both in the Murray-Blessing mail survey and in the face-to-face interviews, decisiveness was *always* seen as a basic trait in top-ranked presidents and rarely judged to be present in low-rated ones.

Clark Clifford, an advisor to both Truman and Lyndon Johnson, once remarked that the public would forgive almost anything in the White House except inaction. President Truman knew this, telling Merle Miller while the latter was working on Truman's oral biography, "The President has to act. That's why the people of the United States elect you."[13] Theodore Roosevelt, who could hardly be charged with being passive, once blurted out his presidential credo: "Get action, do things, . . . create, act."[14] In all the presidential polls, including this one, historians too were apparently affected by this "Don't just stand there, do something!" syndrome. As with character, decisiveness also embraced a host of related attributes that the historians often mentioned in connection with it—determination, tenacity, aggressiveness, confidence, and courage. Almost 81 percent of the historians answering the Murray-Blessing survey believed that presidential success depended as much on tenacity and determination as on the validity of the president's programs. Sixty percent of the respondents declared that they preferred a president who was determined, even to the point of obduracy, to a president who was easily dissuaded.[15] The experiences of several recent chief executives were used to emphasize these points. More than 96 percent stated that Truman's determination was a major asset in making his administration successful. Likewise, 69 percent applauded Lyndon Johnson's tenacity, especially in the area of civil rights and economic affairs. Conversely, many found Carter's personality too bland for the presidency—71 percent gave him poor marks for his apparent indecision.[16]

Despite the strong emphasis placed on decisiveness, it was not always seen as an unalloyed asset, and some subtleties in the historians' views were detected. Nixon, for example, was regarded as decisive and determined, but at critical moments in the wrong way. Action by a president had to be tempered by wisdom and common sense. They also condemned presidential decision-making when it was accompanied by excessive rigidity. Despite the high ranking they gave Woodrow Wilson, 82 percent disagreed with his dogmatic stand in the League of Nations fight. Presidential flexibility as circumstances changed, in contrast to being either too obdurate or too easily swayed, was clearly endorsed by the survey historians.[17] Even so, decisiveness remained for them *the single most important* personality factor.

Where, then, does this whole matter of character and personality and their connection with a successful presidency finally lead? Jerald F. terHorst, President Ford's first press secretary, once observed that success in the White House was largely determined by "the possession of personal attributes that are in public demand at an hour of public need."[18] In general, the Murray-Blessing historians agreed, but they also indicated that because the required attributes changed with circumstances, presidential success could not be evaluated on the basis of character and personality alone. These historians saw certain traits in a president as universally desirable—charisma, intelligence, integrity, and decisiveness. The value of other traits, such as honesty, determination, tenacity, and aggressiveness, depended heavily on the given situation and could be judged as being important only after an administration had passed and its various events had been analyzed. The effectiveness of presidential leadership at any particular moment in time was therefore dependent to a large extent on the *accident* of personality, against which the selection of a president offered no guarantees.[19]

In short, character and personality, although infinitely more important to presidential success than physical appearance, educational training, or previous occupational and political background, could not by themselves ensure a favorable historical verdict or a successful performance in the White House.[20]

F I V E

Presidential Relationships as a Factor in Success

SUCCESS IN THE AMERICAN presidency cannot be evaluated fully without first delineating the major functions of that office and assessing their relative importance. Political scientists have recently combined these functions under a number of headings with rather formidable designations: symbolic leadership; program design and priority setting; crisis management; legislative and political coalition building; program implementation; and oversight of governmental routines.[1] Historians have traditionally described the chief roles of the president in these terms: (1) head of state; (2) executive administrator; (3) commander-in-chief; (4) primary law enforcer; (5) domestic-policy initiator; (6) main foreign-policy planner; (7) party leader; and (8) symbolic national spokesman.

The order of importance in which the Murray-Blessing historians viewed these functions was significant for their final presidential ratings. They placed far in front the role of foreign-policy planner, with domestic-policy initiator behind in second place. Rivaling the latter for the runner-up spot was symbolic spokesman for the nation. Although regarded as being important, the remaining five functions were ranked further down. Of these, head of state was rated highest and party leader lowest, with executive administrator, commander-in-chief, and primary law enforcer sandwiched between.[2]

Since the success of a president in filling these roles often depended on his relationship with other officials or units of government, the nature of that relationship was also of some concern to the survey historians. In some instances they were willing to leave that relationship extremely loose. For example, as party leader dealing with purely party affairs, the president, they asserted, could do anything he could get away with. Although 87 percent claimed that a president had an obligation to try to fulfill his party's platform and campaign promises, an equally large percentage (almost 88 percent) said that his historical rating should not be adversely affected simply because he failed to do so.[3]

Nor did the survey historians believe that it was the president's obligation to keep his party together. Over 80 percent maintained that, after his election, party harmony was not as important as passage of his programs, and more than 86 percent disagreed that party loyalty should take precedence over policy differences. In examining past examples of such differences, for instance, more than 70 percent upheld Cleveland's sticking to his low tariff and sound-money principles despite the catastrophic cost to Democratic party unity in the 1890s, and 91 percent approved of Truman's strong civil rights stand in 1948 even though it split his party wide open.[4]

Both in the personal interviews and in the mail survey, the Murray-Blessing historians declared that the president was superior to his party in every way. Although they admitted that the party was crucial to a president winning an election, they maintained that afterward he was far more important to the party than the party was to him. Presidents, they claimed, should act accordingly, and they rated no president high who easily succumbed to party pressures. In no instance did the historians advocate that party leaders be allowed a veto over presidential actions, and even in the selection of a vice-presidential running mate only a bare majority said the president ought to follow the advice of party leaders or a nominating convention.[5]

The historians' downgrading of the president's role as party leader does not indicate that they believed the president should be above politics. Rather, they seemed to be saying that the presidency is a suprapolitical office whose occupant must seek success through whatever political channels are open to him. In this they agreed with the political scientists, such as Professor Louis W. Koenig, who claim that "the President . . . must build a special coalition for his purpose from both . . . parties [and since] the coalitions keep forming and breaking up as their purpose is achieved . . . the President must develop a new combination [for each new objective]." The point is clear: The president is not and should not be above "practical politics" and should involve himself instead in the widest spectrum of national political activities. In order to fulfill his obligation to his office and the American people, he must sometimes apply the proper sort of political pressure, which according to Professor Koenig involves the use of "blandishments, favors, bargains, compromises, and the application, when necessary, of naked pressure."[6]

The president's relationship with the vice-president, the cabinet, advisors, family, and friends produced a similar hard-line reaction. In every case, the supremacy and inviolability of the presidential office was upheld. Of the president's many governmental contacts, those with the vice-president might be expected to be the most intimate, but historically this has not been so. Except for the very early ones, vice-presidents have been the forgotten men in the presidential equation. Placed on the ticket for geographic balance, age considerations, reward for party loyalty, or to soothe a dissident wing of the party, vice-presidents usually have been isolated and ignored as their records have shown. Look at the modern period alone. By 1940 Franklin Roosevelt and his vice-president, John Nance Garner, had come to such an open break that Roosevelt hinted he would bolt the party rather than see Garner succeed him. Eisenhower never felt comfortable with Nixon as vice-president and more than once intimated that he wished he were off the ticket. Lyndon Johnson handled his vice-president, Hubert Humphrey, in an exceedingly offhand manner and never took him into his confidence. Even Spiro Agnew, one of the laziest and most discredited vice-presidents in history, complained that the office was a "damned peculiar situation to be in." When asked by reporters in his fifth year in office what part he played in the Nixon administration, he replied, "Quite candidly, the President has not defined my role yet."[7]

The responding historians were not bothered by this. They did not regard the vice-president as much of a factor in most presidential administrations. More than two-thirds agreed that a president had the right to set whatever limits he wanted on the involvement of the vice-president, even though a similar number deplored the cavalier way in which Franklin Roosevelt had treated his various running mates. However, as far as could be determined from the information received, the manner in which any of the presidents treated their vice-presidents did not affect their ranking in any significant way.[8]

This neutral attitude toward the vice-presidency carried over to the contributions a vice-president was supposed to make toward an administration's success. The historians split down the middle on whether a president should expect complete loyalty or independent judgment from the vice-president.[9] Although waffling on this matter, more than 70 percent agreed that a former vice-president who becomes president could and should do whatever he determined best without reference or deference to his predecessor.[10] This rule held for *any* president, not just former vice-presidents — a president owned nothing to *any* predecessor. As the answers to certain of the survey's questions showed, a president was not downgraded for ignoring the philosophy or policies of his predecessor as long as he had some of his own. The historians rejected, in particular, the idea that a president should strive to save a former incumbent's reputation or protect him from the normal operations of civil and criminal law. In the case of Ford, for example, more than 68 percent said that he erred badly in pardoning Nixon after he assumed the presidency.[11]

The historians also saw the cabinet as contributing only tangentially to a president's success. Actually, the cabinet was regarded by the historians more as a potential source of trouble than as a benefit to a chief executive's ranking. Almost 89 percent believed that in order to protect his presidential reputation a president had to monitor cabinet members closely and carefully follow their work.[12] Failure to do so, as in the case of Harding and Grant, could have disastrous consequences and contribute heavily toward ruining their historic standing. It is interesting that the historians wanted to see the cabinet become more important than it has been in the past. More than 90 percent indicated a preference for Washington's original use of the cabinet as an advisory body to its subsequent more administrative counterpart. The historians' low estimate of the current importance of the cabinet undoubtedly influenced them to agree that holding a cabinet position was among the least acceptable training grounds for the presidency.[13]

The historical record generally supported these views. Presidents have rarely had a free hand in selecting their cabinets, although some have chosen better cabinets than others. Selected for geographic, ethnic, or political reasons rather than for their loyalty to their chief or agreement with his policies, cabinet members have frequently been more of an embarrassment for the president than an asset. Coolidge's vice-president Charles Dawes, who served in government with some of the best and also some of the most corrupt cabinet members in recent history, once remarked that, when it came to carrying out policy, the members of the cabinet were sometimes the president's worst enemies.[14]

For the modern period, there was no indication that White House cabinet relations figured much in the presidential rankings. In recent years, most cabinet members have had only minimal contact with the White House. Of the modern presidents, only Eisenhower and Carter tried to make the cabinet system work. Nixon ignored his cabinet, and Kennedy openly opposed the idea of using it as a consultative body. Under Johnson, the cabinet, as one aide put it, "became a joke," adding, "It was never used for anything near what could be called presidential listening or consultation."[15] Indeed, in recent years, only the secretaries of Defense, State, and Treasury have continued to maintain contact with the president on more than a routine basis.

Far more than the cabinet, personal advisors to the president (sometimes including the above-mentioned three cabinet members) were viewed by the historians as playing a role in determining administrative success—and with good reason. As far back as Jackson's "Kitchen Cabinet," personal advisors, more than the cabinet, helped formulate administration policy. Only in the modern period, however, has this element been institutionalized. Beginning with Franklin Roosevelt, all recent presidents have placed increasing reliance on this select group of people. Further, the continual creation of advisory units for new and narrowly defined areas of policy (national security, disarmament, women's affairs, etc.) added greatly not only to the size of the White House staff but also to the number of presidential advisors.

Viewing the type, talent, and skill of such advisors as somewhat important in the past, the survey historians indicated that this factor has loomed larger in their thinking concerning modern presidential success. In listing the qualifications a presidential advisor ought to possess, they ranked intelligence at the top, followed by truthfulness, independent judgment, and political experience. Loyalty to the president—a quality most presidents have demanded above all else—placed a very poor last. The historians also agreed that a president should fire an ineffective, corrupt, or untruthful aid immediately upon determining this fact. They claimed, for example, that one of the serious defects of the Nixon administration was his selection of poor advisors, their inferior performance, and his reluctance to get rid of them. They also thought this was true for Carter, and they heavily downgraded other past presidents such as Grant and Harding for the same reason. Conversely, they believed that Franklin Roosevelt chose outstanding talent, and one factor that caused them to upgrade Kennedy's brief term in office was his ability to surround himself with able counselors.[16]

The historians did not care how the advisory machinery of the White House was organized or if the lines of communication were neat and orderly. Their sole test was whether the pattern chosen by the president worked. They regarded the ability of the president to recruit able advisors and to inspire them to high achievement as important factors in ultimate presidential success. The clear message from the survey historians was this: A president ignored selecting and motivating talented advisors both at the peril of good governance and at a risk to his historical standing.

At base, however, the historians considered the president himself to be the most critical ingredient in the whole advisory process. The mail survey historians, as well as those who were interviewed, were firm about this: a president was *directly* responsible for all the activities of his aides and was expected to hold them to strict accountability. Further, *only* the president had the constitutional authority to make decisions—whatever advice he was given—and only he was responsible for the outcome. They agreed that top White House staffers should report only to the president and be personally supervised by him. Sixty-eight percent of the mail respondents supported recent executive moves (including Nixon's) to bring the White House hierarchy under more direct presidential control, and 63 percent disapproved of Carter's post-Watergate decentralized approach to the executive office.[17]

In this sense, the survey historians confirmed the views of some political scientists who see the modern presidency threatened by the growing proliferation and autonomy of the executive departments. In the words of Professor Hugh Heclo, the president is always in danger of being "suffocated by the political and policy technocrats of Washington."[18]

The historians agreed that a president had to keep a tight rein on his staff and at the same time rise above the Byzantine intrigues that sometimes swirl through the White House corridors. Interviewed historians mentioned with particular unhappiness the unremitting "turf" battles which often plague a White House staff and warned that even the most firm-minded president was likely to appear indecisive in this situation. Certainly the staff squabbles of the Carter administration promoted a sense of amateurishness and incompetence, while Taft's inability to keep his top advisors under control deepened the belief that he was weak and inept. On the other hand, Franklin Roosevelt and Kennedy and, earlier, Jefferson and Wilson, benefited from choosing advisors who were both competent and reasonably self-effacing, while Lincoln's masterful handling of his various ambitious and talented advisors still serves as a primary example of clever presidential staff management.

Relatives and friends, unlike advisors, were seen by the historians as having mainly a potentially adverse impact on administration success. With the exception of the First Lady, the historians expected relatives and friends to remain in the background. As one historian wrote in the margin of the survey questionnaire, "His family should shut up and stay at home!" Nearly 70 percent of the mail survey respondents contended, perhaps unrealistically, that the president should monitor closely the activities of his family and friends while he was in the White House, just as he should those of his cabinet and advisors. Further, more than 90 percent stated that he should not put close relatives on the public payroll, and 67 percent claimed that he should not place a family member in a high administrative post, even if that person was qualified. Obviously, presidential actions and the views of the survey historians sometimes differed in these matters. When they did, the effect on presidential rankings was mixed and depended heavily on the performance of the appointees themselves. Placing close family members in high positions apparently had no adverse affect on Kennedy's standing. In Harding's case, the appointment of certain close friends to public office was one of the significant reasons prompting a verdict of failure.[19]

After reviewing all the historians' answers to the various survey questions on a proper presidential relationship with party, party leaders, the cabinet, personal advisors, family, and friends, one fact stood out: The president while in office owed loyalty *to no one* except the American electorate. The survey historians saw the president as being above party, advisors, and cabinet officers. He had nothing to lose and much to gain by changing advisors when dissatisfied and holding them to rigid standards of conduct. Corrupt subordinates were to be cut loose immediately. And with the possible exception of the First Lady, he would be wise to keep his family and close personal friends out of his administration's activities altogether.

The historians treated the president's relationship with the federal bureaucracy in a curiously offhand manner. Not as concerned as political scientists with the structure and workings of the bureaucracy, the historians generally glossed over the president's executive ability, especially in dealing with civil service and patronage matters. Historically, all presidents have fretted over patronage problems, and although the Civil Service Act of 1883 was designed to reduce the patronage load, it created other difficulties. The subsequent growth of the civil service gradually saddled the nation with a politically powerful vested-interest group largely uncontrolled by the president.

It has been said that presidents come and go but the federal bureaucracy remains. Indeed, in many ways the bureaucracy has become a separate branch of government. From the onset of their administrations, most presidents since World War I had difficulty addressing the interrelatedness of many national issues because of this fragmented and feudal bureaucratic structure. Rather than aiding the president, the bureaucracy, with its slowness to act and resistance to change, has often acted as a significant brake on the implementation of presidential policy. Confronting this problem, Lyndon Johnson once remarked, "They geld us first and then expect us to win the Kentucky Derby." Harry Truman put it this way: "I thought I was the President, but when it comes to these bureaucracies, I can't make 'em do a damn thing."[20]

Although it obviously required executive skill of a high order to deal with the orderly management of government and with the federal bureaucracy, the historians regarded this ability in a president as being less necessary than some others. This was just as well, because most of the presidents were not noted for their administrative expertise, and the few who were, like Hoover, were often ill-equipped to handle the political dimensions of the office. The Murray-Blessing historians generally tended to agree with Franklin Roosevelt, who once pooh-poohed the office's administrative aspect by saying, "That is the least part of it. [The presidency] is more than an engineering job, efficient or inefficient."[21] Indeed, of the eight presidential functions, the historians listed executive administrator as only fifth in importance.[22]

In no case was a president singled out by either the mail survey or the interviewed historians for special attention because of his administrative abilities. Perhaps many of these historians knew little about the presidents' expertise in this area, or they may have lacked a common definition of what constituted "administrative ability." In any case, by a strange process of reasoning, the mail survey historians listed the most recently rated presidents in terms of their administrative skill as follows: (1) Franklin Roosevelt, (2) Lyndon Johnson, (3) Kennedy, (4) Eisenhower, (5) Hoover, (6) Truman, (7) Nixon, (8) Carter, and (9) Ford.[23] Their number-one choice, Roosevelt, would have laughed at this listing himself because he once admitted that he was not nearly as good an administrator as other presidents had been. To place Hoover fifth was also not justified. Once more, the historians may have read into the higher-ranked presidents some qualities they did not actually possess.[24]

The presidential relationship with Congress was treated by the historians in a far more serious way. Since Congress has traditionally represented both a constitutional check on presidential action and a necessary partner in translating presidential programs into law, its role in affecting presidential success was indeed sometimes crucially significant.

Actually, the rhetoric and the skills employed by a candidate to win the presidency were not always beneficial or useful when it came to dealing with legislators. Further, even presidents who had served in Congress sometimes found it difficult to win cooperation from that body. Able to erect strong barriers against a president's program, Congress frequently liked to display its independence and exercise its own inherent powers.

President Truman once said, "A President who's any damn good at all makes a lot of enemies." He especially included Congress in this group because he believed that a president who did not joust with Congress was not worth salt. Presidential-congressional tension, Truman claimed, was essential to good government, and cooperation between the two was not always necessary.[25] The Murray-Blessing historians agreed with this and by their answers to the survey's questions also showed that they endorsed the view advanced by Professor Arthur M. Schlesinger, Jr., that the normal relationship between Congress and the president was indeed a state of permanent guerrilla warfare.[26]

The survey historians ranked presidents who adopted an aggressive stance toward Congress higher than those who did not. In no instance did they rank a president high who allowed Congress to steer the ship of state during his tenure. Still, they showed that they did not want Congress to roll over and play dead either. For example, 61 percent stated that the three branches of government (executive, legislative, and judicial) should be kept equal and that the executive (the presidency) should not be permitted to ride roughshod over the other two.[27] Similarly, 91 percent believed that Congress need not pass the president's domestic programs, even though he considered them essential for the welfare of the nation. More than 95 percent agreed that in serious disputes over domestic policy with the president, the Congress did not have to defer to his wishes.[28] On the other hand, 70 percent of these same historians believed that partisan congressional politics should play only a *limited* role in modifying presidential policy in the case of foreign affairs, and a majority would allow a president much wider latitude in forcing his will upon Congress in this area.[29]

The historians were neither clear nor rigid about the correct balance between the powers of the executive and legislative branches and preferred to judge each presidential-congressional confrontation on its own merits. If we can read between the lines, they felt that some cooperation between the Congress and the president was desirable, but the degree could vary widely. As a minimum, they believed that the president's legislative program should be considered by Congress, debated, and voted either up or down, rather than being bottled up in committee or strangled by parliamentary maneuvering. In any case, a "good" relationship between a president and Congress was not a requirement for a successful presidential ranking. Some presidents, such as Cleveland, Truman, and Kennedy, seemed to benefit because of their conflicts with Congress. On the other hand, of the more recent presidents, Ford and Carter were downgraded for their "poor" relationships with Congress.

The Great presidents, in turn, so clearly transcended their Congresses in the minds of the historians that the exact relationship between them seemed unimportant. Some Great, Near Great, and Above Average presidents (e.g., Franklin Roosevelt and Wilson) had excellent relations with their first-term Congresses, only to be harassed by that body in subsequent years. Some (like Kennedy) never had any success with Congress at all. And some (like Eisenhower) maintained a good relationship with that body throughout most of their tenure. The fact remained that the weaker presidents vis-à-vis Congress were generally hurt in the rankings by this congressional factor and the stronger ones were not. Lower-ranked presidents were frequently condemned for their poor congressional relationships; higher-ranked presidents rarely were, even when such a condition existed.

The presidents' relationship with the courts, and especially with the Supreme Court, presented a somewhat different problem. Like the Congress, the courts have traditionally acted as a check on presidential power, and presidents have frequently clashed with them over policies and issues. By their rulings, the courts from time to time have made aspects of presidential programs ineffective. Presidents, on the other hand, have often exercised their constitutional right to determine and alter the composition, and even the size, of the federal courts through their appointive power. Generally, according to the interviewed historians, good presidential appointments to the federal courts (e.g., John Jay by Washington, John Marshall by Jefferson, Oliver W. Holmes by Theodore Roosevelt, Louis Brandeis by Wilson) rebounded to that president's benefit in the rankings; poor appointments did not affect presidential standings one way or the other.[30]

Of the three branches of government, the judiciary was treated by the survey historians as the most sacrosanct. Although they would allow the president maximum flexibility in making court appointments and agreed that he had the right to nominate and place on the bench judges who conformed to his own socioeconomic views, three-quarters of the respondents declared that the president should *in all instances* uphold and enforce court decisions once they were made.[31] Also, 91 percent said the president had no right to demand that the courts "follow the election returns" (i.e., endorse presidential policies simply because the electorate had done so). Viewing the courts as an essential nondemocratic part of government, the historians stuck to these beliefs when tested against specific historical situations. For example, 72 percent declared that Jefferson's attacks on the federal judiciary at the beginning of the nineteenth century were inexcusable. Eighty-nine percent condemned Jackson's defiance of the Supreme Court in 1832 regarding the removal of the Cherokee Indians to lands west of the Mississippi. And despite Franklin Roosevelt's popularity with the historians, 59 percent agreed that he had acted outside his proper prerogatives in trying to pack the Supreme Court in 1937.[32]

Historically, presidents (whether high-ranked or low-ranked) tampered with the federal courts at their peril. Usually only the strongest and most confident presidents attempted to do so, and even they had the scars to show for it (e.g., Jefferson, Jackson, Theodore Roosevelt, Franklin Roosevelt, Truman). Fighting with Congress sometimes had political advantages for a president and even benefited his historical standing. But fighting with the courts was never seen to be an asset by the Murray-Blessing historians. On the other hand, there was no statistical indication that such altercations with the courts adversely affected the ranking of any of the Above Average, Near Great, or Great presidents. Their rankings held *in spite of* and not because of their difficulties with the courts.

Although not an official part of the American constitutional system, the media have often been called the fourth branch of government. Sometimes facilitating the president's exercise of power, but more often providing restraints on it, the media have also played a role in presidential success. Generally, however, this role has had a short-term rather than a long-term historical impact.

Relationships between presidents and the media were adversarial from the beginning. The job of the media was at times to make government more difficult, not necessarily easier, and therefore they rarely served as cheerleaders for the White House.[33] And as most administrations progressed, the gulf between the White House and the media usually increased. After his first two years in office, Kennedy complained he was "reading more but enjoying it less."[34] Even the presidents who gave the impression they like the media (Theodore Roosevelt, Franklin Roosevelt, and Harding) were thin-skinned when it came to taking its criticism. All presidents, when in trouble, regarded the media with suspicion and, in Wild West terms, tended to "draw the wagons close around the White House."

Presidents consistently complained that biased media coverage undermined their ability to govern and that this was a major reason that their public popularity declined as time went by. In order to counteract this, all presidents sought in one way or another to "manage" the news themselves in order to ensure a more favorable image. Early chief executives used "spokesman" newspapers controlled by the administration—a practice that finally died out during Buchanan's tenure. Contemporary presidents have resorted to television and pubic relations experts to explain their policies and polish their images.

In this race to inform the public about the various aspects of an administration, the survey historians sided with the media rather than with the president. Although not held in quite the same esteem as the courts, the media was accorded a privileged position. Indeed, the historians carefully circumscribed the president's relationship to it. They believed that a modern president's duty included holding frequent live news conferences and personally fielding reporters' questions. They admitted that a president might, in the national interest, choose not to answer a given question, but if he elected to answer at all he should tell the truth. Only a bare majority of the historians would permit the White House to create "news leaks" of its own, and a very large minority (46 percent) did not countenance planted news stories by the White House at all. Not only was the thought of peacetime government censorship repugnant to the survey historians, but 57 percent rejected the proposition that a president should ask for media self-censorship in peacetime, even in matters of a sensitive security nature.[35] Further, 85 percent opposed a return to the earlier practice of having an administration-sponsored "spokesman" newspaper. On the other hand, the historians deplored the current trend toward private media monopolies, 56 petcent believing that this had a deleterious impact on modern democratic governance. As for public opinion polls, the historians were ambivalent about how much they should affect a president's performance. Forty-four percent believed the president should be sensitive to such polls, while 56 percent did not think so.[36]

When the historians expressed concern about the damaging effect of the media on the modern presidency, they usually centered their criticism on television. Almost 80 percent agreed that television tended to skew presidential performance from substance to style.[37] When asked about television's impact on specific presidential administrations, the answers were interesting. Fifty-eight percent speculated that Washington's lack of humor and his aristocratic bearing would have made him an unlikely candidate in the current television age. One historian volunteered the thought that Washington would never have survived a Mike Wallace "60 Minutes" segment on Valley Forge. A sizable minority (40 percent) also claimed that Lincoln, because of his ungainly appearance, could never have been elected president if television had existed. Several interviewees maintained that even though Lincoln was elected in 1860, he would not have been renominated or reelected in 1864 if television had brought the Civil War carnage daily into northern living rooms.[38]

Although an interesting exercise, the above involved sheer speculation.

More pertinent, however, was the fact that an overwhelming 90 percent of the historians said television *actually was* a major cause of Nixon's loss to Kennedy in 1960. An equally high percentage (89 percent) listed it as an asset contributing to Kennedy's favorable presidential image. Conversely, slightly more than 50 percent believed that television detracted from the reputation of Lyndon Johnson, and 55 percent selected it as a major factor in prompting him not to run again in 1968. In the case of Nixon, 88 percent saw the media and television as being at least partly responsible for his political downfall.[39]

The historians generally agreed that a president's relationship with the media greatly affected his *contemporary* image. But as important as the media was to a president's immediate political survival, the same historians did not show that it had much effect on his long-term historical standing or on their assessment of presidential performances. For example, Harding, the bottom-ranked president, had one of the best relationships with the press of any chief executive in the nation's history. Conversely, some of the top-ranked presidents were among the most vilified. To press opponents of their day, Washington was a "tyrant"; Jefferson was "Mad Tom"; Jackson, "the worst president ever"; and Lincoln, "the head ghoul in Washington." [40]

Mindful of the ephemeral quality of this media criticism and popular disapproval, the historians indicated that it should not be allowed to go too far. In this regard, the survey's questions concerning the proper reasons for a president's removal from office were germane. In sum, the answers showed that the Murray-Blessing historians were very cautious about presidential removals. They expressed a belief that the Congress should not remove the president because of political or philosophical differences (e.g., Andrew Johnson) even if he had lost the ability to govern. Also, they indicated that having corrupt subordinates, as long as the corruption did not involve the chief executive himself, was no excuse for impeaching and removing him either (e.g., Grant and Harding). According to the historians, only if a president directed his power toward a criminal end or used it to contravene the normal working of the legal system (e.g., Nixon) should he be removed.[41] It is significant that, despite sometimes bitter public and media criticism, only two chief executives in the nation's history have seriously faced being dismissed from office. Although impeached, the one (Andrew Johnson) escaped being convicted; the other (Nixon) resigned before the question of impeachment could be settled and his fate legally determined.

By now it was abundantly clear from the historians' answers to the survey's questions about presidential relationships and about certain presidential functions that they had an uneven impact on the historians' judgments. A president's performance in the roles of party leader and executive administrator did not significantly figure in the ranking process. His relationships with family and friends had even less to do with his historical standing and were of interest only if they caused the president trouble and embarrassment. His contacts with the vice-president and with the cabinet were also only marginally important, and unless these officers proved to be corrupt or decidedly inferior, his historical reputation was not affected much one way or the other. Personal advisors to the president represented a more sensitive area of evaluation, because able ones could reflect positively on a president's standing. Conversely, they could also detract from the historians' view of a president's success. His relationship with Congress was seen as a test of his political skill, and a certain amount of progress was expected in this area. But cooperation with Congress was not necessarily a prerequisite to a good rating. Finally, the president's interaction with the courts and the media mainly had a short-term impact on his presidency and did not presage the nature of his ultimate historical standing.

In the final analysis, the historians' answers to all the survey's questions thus far demonstrated that even the most adroit and skillful presidential interactions with other officials, the bureaucracy, the Congress, the media, or the courts could not offset crippling defects in a president's overall character. The historians emphasized at every opportunity that such personality qualities as decisiveness, intelligence, and integrity were much more influential in determining a president's eventual historical reputation. More important, both in their answers on the survey questionnaire and in the face-to-face interviews, they demonstrated that even the most desirable character and personality traits and the finest official relationships did not prompt a decision for true greatness unless these were joined by outstanding and lasting administrative achievements.

Administration Achievements
and Presidential Greatness

NO PRESIDENT WHO WAS CONSIDERED Great or Near Great by the Murray-Blessing historians lacked substantial administration achievements. All such presidents were imbued with a sense of mission, a desire to accomplish, a zeal to make things happen. That they were sometimes blocked in their efforts was not as important as the fact that they continued to run with the ball even when they were being tackled. In all these cases, presidential "activeness" was a precondition for administration achievement, just as it also served as a showcase for presidential courage, confidence, tenacity, and determination. All the Great and Near Great presidents were both action-oriented and "progressive." As used here, "progressive" means a willingness to promote fundamental change and is not to be confused with the more technical historical term associated with the Progressive Era. While much may be said for the maintenance of the status quo, history has tended to immortalize leaders who have not been primarily concerned with maintaining the status quo—and the rankings of the survey historians proved it. Washington, who in many ways was a political conservative, was the guiding spirit of one of the world's most successful revolutions. Lincoln wanted to preserve the Union, but in pursuing that goal, altered forever the sociopolitical patterns of the American people. Franklin Roosevelt set out to save the American capitalistic system but in the process recast the nation's economic life. Such leadership usually resulted in expanding the role of the federal government through broadening the political base of the nation's citizens, expanding and strengthening economic opportunities, providing greater social equality, and protecting the many against the few. The means most often used were programs of political, economic, and social reforms which forever connected their sponsors' names with significant trends or periods in the nation's history—Jefferson with Agrarian democracy; Jackson with Jacksonian democracy; Theodore Roosevelt with Progressivism; Wilson with the New Freedom; Franklin Roosevelt with the New Deal.

In the eyes of the survey historians, central to this development was the role of the president as the symbolic spokesman for the nation. Ranked third in importance in the list of presidential functions, being symbolic spokesman for the nation was considered by the survey respondents to be only slightly below domestic-policy initiator and foreign-policy planner. As historian Allan Nevins put it, "We need someone who every morning will himself awake, and thus make the rest of us awake, to the rumble of a lofty battle."[1] Indeed, the president's ability to set the national agenda and then point the public in that direction through the skillful use of imagery and rhetoric was often the first step along the road to ensuring himself a solid place in history.

The survey historians found this kind of leadership present in all the Great and Near Great presidents. Such leadership exhibited a capacity for creative innovation and an imagination that was fired by a clear vision of the future. They also saw these men exercising a high degree of "moral leadership." According to the historians, moral leadership embraced a number of significant qualities: deep commitment, humaneness, sensitivity to public needs, and the ability to inspire. The latter was considered especially necessary for a great president. The ability to inspire involved first the ability to explain and then the power to arouse. Even if the causes of a problem were complex, and solutions were extremely difficult, the historians expected a great president to be able to reduce it all to terms simple enough for the average citizen to understand.

Thus, a great president had to be an excellent communicator and a teacher to the nation. At the same time, he had to have the ability to summon his followers to action and to higher achievements than they would have otherwise thought possible. Wilson's rhetoric, for example, was uplifting and one of his strongest weapons in dealing with the public and Congress. And certainly no president surpassed Lincoln in the use of language for the expression of feelings and hopes for the future. Franklin Roosevelt frequently proved that words were extremely important—his first inaugural address was an excellent example. As Clement Attlee once said of Winston Churchill, "Words at great moments of history are deeds."[2]

It might seem at this point that the Murray-Blessing historians agreed with pollster George Gallup's contention that people "judge a man by his goals, by what he is trying to do, and not necessarily by what he accomplishes."[3] This was not true of these historians. Idealism, a clear agenda, the excellent use of rhetoric, and lofty goals may have influenced them to place a few presidents in the Above Average category rather than in the Average group, but it did not cause them to raise any to the level of greatness unless accompanied by solid achievements. In recent years both the public's desire for a "quick fix" to national problems and the White House's use of public relations gimmicks have beguiled the electorate into sometimes believing that mere presidential incantations can substitute for concrete action. Also, there is a modern relativist tendency to accept the idea that achievement is largely in the eye of the beholder. In evaluating past presidents, the historians resisted all such tendencies. After applying various tests to the Schlesinger polls of 1948 and 1962, one study found that a rating of administration accomplishments and the Schlesinger rankings of the presidents conformed very closely to each other.[4] Of *all* the various factors uncovered in the Murray-Blessing survey, administration accomplishments and presidential rankings also seemed the most clearly connected.

In analyzing administration achievements, the survey historians treated domestic and foreign affairs differently. In the years before the twentieth century, domestic affairs occupied the more important place in their evaluation of presidential performances. The reverse was true for the years since 1945. In all time periods, however, the historians allowed the president much less leeway in dealing with domestic affairs than with foreign matters. This was in part because the checks built into the American system could operate more effectively in the domestic field than in the foreign field, and in part because a president was expected to be more "open" in his handling of the domestic affairs. In any case, when domestic and foreign problems competed in any time period, foreign-policy issues were regarded more seriously by the historians. This fact, as much as any other, helps explain why wartime presidents were generally ranked higher than peacetime ones. In the present survey, no wartime president was rated lower than a high Average (McKinley, eighteenth).

The historians saw most of the significant domestic achievements of any administration revolving around four distinct themes: socioeconomic policy, federal versus state and local concerns, enforcement of the law, and the expansion of human civil rights. In almost all clashes between local and federal responsibility, the historians favored the federal side. For example, they condemned Jackson (despite his high ranking) for his use of the state banks as the repository for federal funds; they applauded John Q. Adams and his plan for national aid to transportation and to a national university; they supported Lyndon Johnson's use of federal monies for local pollution control; and they agreed with Nixon's anti-inflation policy of wage and price restrictions. At base, however, the historians remained flexible in judging most socioeconomic policies, choosing to judge them on whether they met the needs of the day and whether they were successful or not.[5]

Not so with regard to law enforcement. Here the historians were rather precise in their attitude. Although they ranked the president's role as primary law-enforcer next to last among his various tasks, the historians did not regard it lightly. They apparently ranked this function low because they saw so little room for maneuvering by the chief executive in this area. From their point of view, a president could not choose to exercise this function; he *had* to exercise it as an integral part of his job. Law enforcement was a presidential duty, not an option.[6]

Hoover once claimed that "the very core of the Presidency was enforcement of the laws."[7] All presidents have regarded themselves as the chief enforcer of the law, although their enthusiasm for upholding certain laws sometimes lagged. The survey historians believed that *in every instance* the chief executive should enforce the law, no matter what his person feelings. An overwhelming three-quarters of the respondents said that the president must enforce the law even if in his judgment it was in the national interest not to do so. Further, a president had to abide by the law himself, regardless of his own moral or ethical position.[8] Briefly put, the historians saw the United States as a government of laws with the president also being bound by them. This dictum applied to *all* presidents, and for them not to abide by it was to run the risk of graver consequences than a poor historical rating. Not only was Nixon's presidential standing hurt by this fact, but almost two-thirds of the survey respondents declared that he should have served a jail sentence if he was guilty of the Watergate charges. Ford, similarly, incurred the displeasure of more than two-thirds of the historians because, by pardoning Nixon before a trial, they did not believe he had enforced the laws equally.[9]

Enforcement of the laws, however, was not without its ambiguous side, especially when the right of dissent was involved. For example, although a majority of the historians approved of Washington's tough handling of the Whiskey Rebellion in 1794, more than 90 percent opposed John Adams's method of suppressing dissent through the Alien and Sedition Acts of 1798. Likewise, 86 percent condemned Cleveland's use of troops in the Pullman Strike of 1894, and an even higher percentage believed he was too harsh in his treatment of Coxey's Army in that same year. A similar large group gave Lyndon Johnson only fair-to-poor marks for his handling of internal dissent in the middle 1960s. Hoover too was criticized for the way he reacted to the Bonus March of 1932. On the other hand, a majority of the historians supported Lincoln's suspension of the writ of habeas corpus during the Civil War, and more than 93 percent upheld Jackson's threatened use of force in the South Carolina Nullification Controversy of 1832–1833.[10]

When asked the question directly, a majority of the survey historians approved of a president using whatever force was necessary to halt the imminent overthrow of government. Within certain limits, they would also allow him to use force to uphold the civil or voting rights of citizens and to protect public and private property. Still, one out of ten historians indicated that they would not allow the president to use force to suppress internal dissent of any kind.[11]

When scaled, these survey results showed that the closer internal dissent came to the actual overthrow or dissolution of government (e.g., Whiskey Rebellion, Nullification Controversy, and Civil War), the higher the percentage of historians who approved force. But when the issue revolved mainly around freedom of expression or differences of opinion on socioeconomic matters (Bonus March, Coxey's Army, labor strikes and disputes) only a minority supported it. Those areas where the historians believed presidential force could be used properly were (in order of their legitimacy): overthrow of government, the protection of civil rights, and the protection of public and private property. It is interesting that the historians considered the protection of public and private property to be the *least* acceptable reason for using force—for this is the area where presidents have customarily used it. Cleveland and Hoover were two presidents whose historical reputations suffered as a result.

As one moved into the modern period, the forcefulness and skill with which a president handled the troubling issue of civil rights became increasingly significant in the historians' assessment of his domestic-policy success.[12] Civil rights and their relationship to presidential performance affected the historians' thinking only to a minor degree when analyzing events in the pre–Civil War period. On matters involving slavery, for example, the respondents remained historically oriented and did not attempt to read contemporary attitudes on race back into that time period, even though they generally condemned actions that prevented North-South compromise and supported evolutionary and nonviolent moves for slavery's elimination or curtailment. Still, presidents of that era were not downgraded because of their own connection with the "peculiar institution" (Washington, Jefferson, Madison, Monroe, Jackson, and Polk all owned slaves). In treating the period immediately following the Civil War, the majority of historians viewed civil rights not predominately as an ethical or moral issue but instead as a judicial and legal problem involving the conflicting police power of the states and the federal government. [13]

In judging the presidents since 1945, the historians regarded the expansion and protection of civil rights as a critical part of an administration's achievements. Truman's Near Great rating evidently rested to some extent on his initiatives and courage in this area. While a large number of the historians believed that Eisenhower acted too slowly in the Little Rock crisis of 1957, they overwhelmingly approved of the final outcome. In spite of the Vietnam disaster, Lyndon Johnson was accorded a high rating mainly because of his civil rights legislation, more than 95 percent of the historians declaring it to be the best part of his administration. [14] Even Carter, although downgraded for many other reasons, gained sympathy from the historians for his insistence on injecting civil rights (i.e., human rights) considerations into American foreign policy. [15]

Foreign affairs were always viewed by the historians as being an important yardstick for measuring presidential success. However, the movement of the nation toward world-power status in the twentieth century, and the changing thrust of the presidency itself, prompted them to give foreign affairs increasing weight as they moved into the contemporary period. Asked whether they preferred a modern president who was skilled in domestic matters or one who was skilled in foreign affairs, the larger number selected the latter. As noted elsewhere, they listed foreign-policy planning as the *foremost* presidential function. Head of State, which they ranked fourth in the list of presidential duties, was closely associated in their minds with foreign policy because of the modern practice of summitry. Indeed, both in the interviews and by their answers to the survey's questions, the historians stated that accomplishments in the foreign field represented *the single most important* factor in the ranking of presidents. [16]

President watchers have long maintained that a president has his greatest opportunity for constructive unilateral action in the area of foreign affairs. Presidents themselves have endorsed this assessment—such recent ones as Truman, Eisenhower, and Nixon declaring foreign policy was the most important aspect of their administrations. Certainly modern presidents have expended more energy on foreign affairs than on domestic matters, devoting as much as two-thirds of their time to this area. [17]

Perhaps it was because the presidents had a freer hand in foreign policy that they were so attracted to it; perhaps too it was because foreign affairs represented a more dramatic aspect of the presidency. In any case, the presidents *did* have greater powers of initiative in the foreign field and *were* subjected to fewer restraints than in the domestic area. A president's advantages here were considerable: he set the foreign-policy agenda; he directed diplomatic negotiations and largely monopolized the sources of information about foreign problems; and, as commander-in-chief, he controlled emergency action if it had to be taken.

Secretary of State Henry Kissinger once told the Senate Foreign Relations Committee: "Every president has a right to conduct foreign policy in a way that helps him most."[18] Kissinger undoubtedly meant by this that what helped the president in this area also presumably helped the nation, and vice versa. Presidents have acted on this basis and have shown a fairly consistent record of power aggrandizement in the foreign-policy area. It is little wonder that in analyzing the emergence of the so-called imperial presidency, Arthur M. Schlesinger, Jr., found the expansion of presidential power in the foreign area to be its major ingredient.[19] Little wonder too that the Murray-Blessing historians, in rating the presidents, saw the qualities of intelligence, decisiveness, confidence, determination, and courage, which they much admired, most clearly expressed in presidential reactions to foreign crises or situations.

The survey historians generally opposed rigid controls on presidential freedom of action in foreign affairs, even in regard to the exercise of the war powers, seeing the latter problem not so much one of structure and definition as one of wisdom and clearheaded decision-making on the part of the chief executive. They clearly did not want the president to turn over the responsibility for foreign affairs to Congress; indeed, they expected the president to be sound enough in his foreign-policy decision to carry Congress with him.[20] As mentioned earlier, the majority of respondents believed that Congress should play only a limited role in modifying presidential foreign policy, even though the danger of presidential excess always existed.[21]

In the end, if presidential excesses in the foreign field were to be avoided, it would be because of the nature of the presidential character. Foreign affairs, and especially wartime crises, were considered by the historians to be major tests of presidential wisdom, restraint, political skill, and integrity. The historians agreed that the president needed to pursue a pragmatic day-to-day course of action—one that was suited to the immediate requirements of the situation. But they also agreed that the final result should be in keeping with the best moral and ethical traditions of American society.[22] Within limits, the means used by a president to achieve that final result should also be morally and ethically acceptable.[23]

Theodore Roosevelt provided the best example on the survey question-naire of a chief executive seizing the initiative in foreign policy, bypassing Congress when he thought necessary, and selecting a variety of means to arrive at satisfactory ends. Roosevelt helped instigate rebellions, engineered secret understandings with foreign powers, settled wars, even sent the fleet around the world while daring Congress to refuse to appropriate the funds to bring it back. The survey historians showed by their answers that they were not always pleased by such actions, but they did not question Roosevelt's right to act thus—especially because he was successful at it. His ranking of fifth says more about his overall foreign-policy success than about the validity of any one of his foreign-policy actions.[24]

The problem of overall success versus the specific situation in foreign policy was obviously a thorny one for the historians because they often voted one way on a president and another on his individual deeds. Wanting the president to be forceful in the foreign-policy area, the respondents nonetheless held to a more passive and noninterventionist ideal. The paradox was glaring, yet the attitudes expressed were remarkably consistent. For example, the majority of the historians believed Madison should not have allowed the nation to go to war in 1812; they approved of Van Buren not aiding the Canadian rebels in 1837 to overthrow English rule; they disagreed with Polk's unilateral action in sending the army to the Texas boundary in 1846; they believed that Monroe should have censured Jackson's military filibus-tering activities in Florida in 1818; they supported Grant in not helping the Cubans toward independence following the 1873 Virginius Affair; they agreed with Cleveland's rejection of Hawaiian annexation following that island's revolution in 1893; they disapproved of McKinley's acquisition of the Philippines in 1898; they approved of Kennedy not giving aid to the Bay of Pigs rebels in 1961; and they believed that Ford should not have used force in the *Mayaguez* incident in 1975. The only cases offered in the survey which ran counter to those were the historians' approval of Truman's intervention in Korea in 1950, and a belief that Carter should have given arms or other aid in 1979 to the Afghan anti-Soviet rebels.[25]

This general noninterventionist attitude was also seen in the historians' reactions to several hypothetical questions posed by the survey on the correct limits of American overseas involvement. No more than 37 percent would allow the president in peacetime to intervene militarily in the affairs of another nation, even when a vital American defense interest in a strategic area was threatened. Less than 9 percent would allow it if only an American economic interest was endangered. Only 7 percent would countenance military intervention to overthrow an anti-U.S. military dictatorship, and less than 3 percent would permit the use of military force to overturn a popularly established anti-U.S. government. Only one-quarter of the historians approved of even nonmilitary intervention to eliminate a popularly established anti-U.S. government, and less than half (43 percent) endorsed other-than-military intervention to protect a vital American defense interest in a strategic area. Nearly one out of five historians rejected U.S. intervention in the affairs of another state in peacetime *for any reason* and *by any means*.[26]

The important word here was not such much "intervention" as "military"; the phrase "popularly established" was also a key to the historians' thinking. In these hypothetical cases, the historians displayed both a pacifist (nonmilitary) and a pro-democratic (popularly established) bent. Their attitude toward aggressive presidential action in this hypothetical realm, as in the actual historical situations, remained uniformly negative.

Yet their rankings of the presidents still confirmed that, as a group, they most admired the chief executives who acted contrary to such pacifistic and noninterventionist beliefs. Even the survey historians whom we ascertained were the least aggressive in foreign-policy matters (20 percent of the sample) did not differ from those who were the most aggressive (also 20 percent of the sample) in their rankings of the Great and Near Great presidents, except for Truman. Truman was ranked only eleventh (Above Average) by the least aggressive historians, instead of eighth (Near Great) as in the case of the most aggressive group. Below the Near Great category, a number of presidential rankings were significantly affected by this least aggressive versus most aggressive split, illustrating that foreign policy was indeed a major determinant in the historians' view of presidential performances. For example, the difference in rankings between these two groups on Carter was nine places, on Polk seven, on Ford four. It is interesting that Nixon was ranked at the very bottom (thirty-sixth) by the least aggressive historians while the most aggressive ranked him thirty-first, raising him out of the Failure category into the Below Average group (see Appendix 10).

Returning again to the responses of the survey historians as a whole, it appeared that the final yardstick used by a majority of the historians was not what they thought personally about the validity of any particular foreign venture itself, but whether the total foreign-policy program of a president was successful and was, in the long run, in the interests of the nation. Success in the foreign field, after all, could not occur without some risks. Strong and aggressive presidents assumed such risks by expanding the power and influence of the United States, often at the expense of other countries. As long as such presidential action did not contravene commonly accepted moral and ethical standards, the results were what really counted. Thus, despite the personally held biases of many historians, it was almost always helpful to a president's ranking to have successfully initiated aggressive foreign-policy moves.

Wary as most of the survey historians were about presidential adventurism in the foreign field, they were firm in their support of the president's powers as commander-in-chief. Although listed only sixth in importance among the eight presidential functions, the role of commander-in-chief was regarded by them in much the same light as being the primary law enforcer. Being commander-in-chief was a task the president had to perform when the occasion arose; he had no real choice in the matter. While the historians might argue as to the correct balance between the president and Congress over the war powers, they left no doubt that the president had absolute jurisdiction over the armed forces, the armed forces' civilian secretaries, and the military chiefs. They agreed that the president had the right to act directly in all military situations and that he could issue any orders to any military officers in the field (a near-unanimous 98 percent, for example, supported Truman's removal of MacArthur). Further, they held the president directly accountable for the success or failure of military ventures even though, as we have seen, they did not require that he have any military experience.[27]

The nation has been fortunate that all of its chief executives who filled the role of commander-in-chief considered the military to be the servant of civilian policy. Of the thirty-nine presidents (including Reagan), twenty had military experience, with ten (as mentioned earlier) holding the rank of general at one time or another. Yet none even so much as hinted that the military should be anything but subservient to civilian control. It is also interesting that many of these men were not the nation's more aggressive presidents in foreign policy but the less aggressive ones.

Not all the presidents, of course, had the occasion to exercise fully the duties of commander-in-chief because of the tranquillity of the times in which they served. Most of the wartime presidents, however, acquitted themselves in this role quite well. Polk's able handling of the Mexican War was one of the highlights of his administration. Lincoln, after a very shaky start, proved to be an able commander-in-chief.[28] Wilson felt uncomfortable in this position in World War I, yet he appointed excellent men to top military positions and, like Lincoln before him, used a forceful assumption of executive power to justify an unusually broad scope of presidential actions, not all of which were militarily related. Franklin Roosevelt gave a virtuoso performance as commander-in-chief after the United States entered World War II. As for Truman, his firing of MacArthur in 1951 and his firm hold over military strategy during the Korean War brilliantly reenforced the principle of civilian supremacy over the military.[29]

In evaluating the various data relating to administration achievements, one additional factor constantly appeared that could not be easily dismissed. Multiple terms in the White House unquestionably had an important effect both on administration accomplishments and on the survey historians' judgment of relative presidential success. After all, chief executives who served longer had a greater opportunity to build up substantial administration achievements than those who experienced shorter tenures. It is not surprising that greatness and longevity in the office usually went hand in hand. The top eight presidents (those rated Great and Near Great) occupied the presidential office a total of sixty-three years; the bottom eight held it for only thirty-eight years. Of the top eight, only Lincoln had less than two terms in the White House (actually, Truman's tenure was only seven years and 283 days); of the bottom eight, only Grant served two full terms. It is interesting in this connection that the historians indicated they were overwhelmingly opposed to limiting the presidential office to one term, as has been proposed from time to time, and they favored a president serving more than two terms if he desired and could get elected.[30]

After completing an analysis of the various data gleaned from the face-to-face interviews and from the mail historians' answers to the Murray-Blessing survey, *outstanding* administration achievements in domestic, foreign, and military affairs emerged as a *sine qua non* of presidential greatness. Even so, the answers to other questions on the survey showed that administration accomplishments alone could not prompt such a rating from the historians. The failing presidents now served to demonstrate the point. The Grant, Harding, and Nixon presidencies were not without their achievements, certainly sufficient under normal circumstances to have kept them out of the lowest category. But in these three cases the positive aspects were overshadowed by exceedingly poor appointments, by scandal and corruption, and by serious presidential personality and character flaws. For Buchanan and Andrew Johnson, "the times" (immediately before and after the Civil War)

joined with their singular lack of political skill, their indecisiveness, or their
faulty decision-making to cause a verdict of failure. In all of these cases, the
chief executive lost (or was in the process of losing) the ability to govern.

That outstanding administration achievements came to the fore as a
key ingredient in presidential greatness was not unexpected. But what was
less obvious, and now proven to be equally significant, was that in the
process of building these achievements a president had the *best* opportunity
to show off the character and personality traits that the historians had ear-
marked as critical and not display those the historians deplored. Great presidents successfully blended their personalities *and* their administration
achievements into a composite in which these various ingredients reenforced
and highlighted each other.[31]

The three top-rated presidents named by the survey historians illustrated
this beautifully. Holding office in different time periods, operating under
different domestic and foreign circumstances, and facing entirely different
social and economic problems, each of them in their own way displayed all
the major essentials the survey historians sought in greatness. Washington
produced an administration filled with significant legislation and executive
precedents and surrounded himself with able lieutenants who helped put the
new nation on a firm footing. His administration added a Bill of Rights to
the Constitution, established credit at home and abroad, and encouraged
commerce and manufacturing. He squelched a serious insurrection in Pennsylvania, fought off the Indian in the transmontane frontier, and set up a
lasting policy for the disposition of public lands. His administration secured
the removal of British troops from the Old Northwest and obtained transit
rights on the Mississippi from the Spanish. In accomplishing this record,
he displayed forthrightness, firmness, farsightedness, determination, and
decisiveness, all tempered with restraint and wisdom.

Franklin Roosevelt was president 150 years later and, like Washington,
his contributions to the nation were a product of what he was and what he
did. Roosevelt was a great politician, a great innovator, a great humanitarian,
and a great showman. He was a skillful judge of talent and a manipulator
of people, infusing his administration with exceptional advisors and public
servants. He was a master communicator and sensitive to the use of words
to convey ideas and to stir the spirit. His confidence, his optimism, and his
determination were important to a nation beset first by economic depression
and then by global war. Using aggressive presidential leadership, he initiated
sweeping social and economic reforms, revitalized the American economic
system, and then put it to work in the struggle against totalitarianism. An

able commander-in-chief, Roosevelt led the military coalition that won World War II and was clearly the dominant figure in the wartime conferences. Although there is still argument over the success of his wartime diplomacy, certainly not the least of his accomplishments was the creation of the United Nations. His impact on later administrations, on the political philosophy of the nation, and on world history itself was immense.

But it was Lincoln, more than any other president, who personified true greatness for the survey historians. Perhaps the stirring events of 1861–1865 would have made any president memorable, yet Lincoln brought to those years a special flavor. His strength of character, his humaneness, his humor, and his common sense were qualities that were sorely needed at a time of gravest national peril. The dominant figure of his day, Lincoln managed his subordinates with a combination of patience and firmness. He was successful in uniting the North behind him, and he laid the foundation for the ultimate recementing of the Union. He prevented the intervention of foreign powers in the civil conflict and moved cautiously toward the emancipation of slaves and a refashioning of the nation's social, political, and economic fabric. He wielded the powers of the president with authority and held with bulldog tenacity to the goal of preserving the Union. As commander-in-chief, he took responsibility for the strategy that led to victory, and he gave meaning to all the terrible bloodshed by putting into words the ideals for which the war was being fought. This man of "velvet steel" was great in spirit, in humility, in capacity for growth, in forgiveness, and in political instincts. For all such reasons Lincoln remained for the survey historians the classic symbol of American democratic leadership and of presidential presence in an hour of supreme crisis.

SEVEN

Reactions to Presidential Rankings and Presidential Performances

PUBLICATION OF THE FIRST SCHLESINGER POLL in 1948 generated not only a surprising amount of public interest but also a considerable number of complaints. The largest number of complaints received by the Harvard professor came from those who opposed the experts ranking Franklin Roosevelt so high. After his second poll in 1962, Schlesinger was again bombarded with protests, this time the most numerous centered around Truman being rated as Near Great while Eisenhower was placed near the bottom of the Average group.[1]

When the first ranking results of the present study appeared in *Parade Magazine* in late 1982, we also were deluged by an avalanche of complaints about how wrong the historian experts were. Such protests, sometimes accompanied by multipage letters, ranged all over the lot, indicating once more not only a wide public interest in rating the presidents but also the differing criteria used by people to assess those who have held that office. Although no one objected to the premier position of Lincoln, numerous protestors did not like Washington being placed below Franklin Roosevelt. Some did not want Roosevelt put in the top three at all. Kennedy and Lyndon Johnson also had their detractors who wanted them placed farther down on the list. A number still complained that Truman was ranked too high and that Eisenhower was too low. And so it went. A man from Worcester, Massachusetts, wrote, "I always considered Coolidge our best president." One Californian asserted, "Nixon is the only man among them." The most succinct letter read:

Dear Dr. Murray:
Regarding your listing of presidents. Pfft!![2]

The most persistent general public criticism made against the present survey was that the historians were too Democratically oriented and too liberally biased in their opinions. The same charge was leveled against both Schlesinger polls. Was there really a Democratic party bias shown by these historians? True, we did not ask the political affiliation of the respondents in the survey, fearing that this might cause some of them not to participate. But we did endeavor to get at the matter another way. Since 1856 (the year of the first presidential election in which the modern Republican party participated) and before Reagan, the Democratic party has elected eight presidents for thirteen terms (fifty-two years); the Republican party has elected thirteen presidents for eighteen terms (seventy-two years). Of the ten top-ranked presidents, the party lineup was as follows:

Republican	Federalist/ Republican	Jefferson-Jackson Democrat	Democrat
Lincoln	Washington	Jefferson	F. Roosevelt
T. Roosevelt	J. Adams	Jackson	Wilson
			Truman
			L. Johnson

If the top thirteen presidents were to be included, Eisenhower's name should be added to the first column and Kennedy's to the last.

In this party connection, it was interesting that the lowest-ranked era for presidents (pre–Civil War) was dominated by Jacksonian Democrats. The series of three worst presidents in the nation's history was Fillmore (Whig), Pierce (Democrat), and Buchanan (Democrat). The next worst was Andrew Johnson (a Union Democrat), Grant (Republican), and Hayes (Republican). Conversely, the best three consecutive presidents were Washington, John Adams, and Jefferson; next came Franklin Roosevelt, Truman, and Eisenhower; and finally Theodore Roosevelt, Taft, and Wilson. Three of the latter were Republican, three were Democrat, two were Federalist, and one was a Jefferson-Jackson Democrat.[3]

If the party lineup of the presidents in the listing above does suggest a Democratic party bias (whatever the historians' actual party affiliations might have been), was there a liberal bias? If "liberal" means to favor the general supremacy of federal authority over local authority and to support central government intervention in the socioeconomic process on behalf of minorities and the less fortunate, then a large majority of the survey's sample were liberal. We estimated from the answers to certain survey questions and from the oral interviews that slightly more than 25 percent of the respondents favored massive government intervention in the socioeconomic realm, another 60 percent supported significant intervention, and less than 15 percent were opposed to such action. From the survey answers and from the results of the face-to-face interviews, it was evident that a large majority of the historians supported a broad spectrum of welfare programs to aid the needy, endorsed graduated tax scales benefiting the nonwealthy, favored low protectionism as opposed to either free trade or high tariffs, and disagreed strongly with the supply-side or "trickle down" theory of economic progress.[4]

As in the case of the least aggressive versus the most aggressive historians on foreign policy, these liberal versus conservative attitudes on domestic issues produced some sharp differences both in the individual ratings and in the rankings of a number of presidents. In this instance, the names (though not the specific rankings) of the top eight presidents remained the same. But among the bottom-ranked presidents, Nixon was again treated differently. Liberals placed him thirty-fifth, just above Harding, while conservatives (like the aggressive historians on foreign policy) elevated him out of the Failure category to thirty-first. Again, it was in the middle groups that presidential rankings were most dramatically affected, indicating that domestic issues were indeed only a step behind foreign policy in influencing the historians' view of presidential performance. For example, the ranking difference between the liberal group and the conservative group on Eisenhower was three places, on Hoover four, and on Lyndon Johnson four. In the case of both Kennedy and Carter the difference was a whopping seven places (see Appendix 11).

These Murray-Blessing findings cast grave doubt on a 1970 study that purported to analyze the effect of a liberal-conservative bias in the two Schlesinger polls. The results of that study were not entirely satisfactory because of the relatively large number of historians who were unwilling to state whether they were "liberal" or "conservative." Even so, enough data was allegedly gleaned to suggest that there was no liberal-conservative division in the ranking of presidents. According to this 1970 study, liberal historians tended to admire flexibility and idealism in a president more than conservatives; similarly, liberals tended to view idealistic and flexible presidents as more prestigious than their less flexible and less idealistic counterparts. Yet both liberal and conservative historians used administration accomplishments as the key factor in assessing presidential performance— something the present survey also confirmed. However, unlike the present survey, the 1970 study stated that the rankings of the presidents by these two groups of historians did not materially differ.[5]

Leaving the question of conservative and liberal bias aside, the Murray-

Blessing survey revealed one indisputable fact about the responding historians: The overwhelming majority identified with a strong, active presidency.
They did not want a weak or messenger-boy chief executive. As a result of
Vietnam and Watergate, they were now more acutely aware of the drastic
consequences of faulty presidential decisions and mistakes than they were in
the 1950s and 1960s. Even so, they did not recoil against continued strength
in the White House. The vast majority still admired active presidents, fearing
only the abuse and not the use of presidential power. Neither the power nor
even the "imperial" tendencies of the modern presidency bothered them as
much as the goals and purposes to which this power and these tendencies
were directed.[6]

The Murray-Blessing survey revealed yet another fact about these historians: Throughout, they maintained a basic humility about their ability
to judge presidential performances. This was not because they lacked faith
in the methodology of their discipline or in their own discriminating capabilities. Rather, it stemmed from the realization that the variables were
often too many to comprehend, master, or synthesize completely. In one of
the survey's most revealing questions, we asked the historians if they agreed
with President Kennedy's assertion, made at the time he was invited to
participate in the second Schlesinger poll in 1962, that unless you were in
the president's shoes and knew all the possible alternatives at the moment
of decision, you could not judge his actions properly. It is significant that
more of the historians agreed with Kennedy than disagreed with him.[7]

Nonetheless, historians *have* judged presidential performances, and so
also in its own way has the American public. Indeed, all citizens act as their
own historians at least once every four years when they are forced to follow
their own best judgment with regard to performance in the White House.
Every vote cast for a president of the United States carries with it either the
hope for a successful performance or the endorsement of one. Indeed, most
Americans look upon a presidential campaign and voting for a president
much more seriously than choosing a governor or a senator. As one recent
pollster said, "Very few cast a frivolous vote; the stakes are too high."[8]

The public wants a president to succeed, yet, like the historians, they
hold him to high and rigid standards. The president becomes a convenient
handle by which the average citizen can grasp the complexities of government, and they demand of him a superhuman effort. They also expect him
to display the finest qualities in the human experience and feel cheated if
he does not measure up. Many Americans may not be able to define exactly
what it is they want in a president, but, like the professional historians,

they maintain that they can recognize it when they see it. Also, just like the historians, they want quite different things simultaneously. The presidency, more than any other office, contains seemingly irreconcilable paradoxes that, at base, point up the American ambivalence toward presidential power. Like the historians, the public wants a strong and active president, but it also reveres the multiple checks and balances that prevent a president from becoming too powerful. Moreover, the public wants a president who is accountable yet will act and think independently; he is expected to speak for all the people, yet his campaign is bankrolled by vested interests; he is to represent the majority yet advance the cause of minorities; he is the custodian of past traditions, yet is expected to be the architect of the future; he is to remain above politics and yet be a consummate politician.[9]

Unlike with the historians, only a few polls have been taken to discover how the public actually feels about the presidency. Those that do exist show that it demands much of a president in the way of character. The public's requirements of charisma, honesty, integrity, and decisiveness are the same as those endorsed by the professional historians. In addition, opinion pollsters have found that "trust" is a particularly critical ingredient in a chief executive as far as the public is concerned. The Yankelovich polls conducted for *Time* magazine almost always included the question "Is he a leader you can trust?" In brief, the public apparently looks for four things in a president: (1) integrity of character, (2) trust and assurance, (3) action, and (4) legitimacy (defined as respectability in the office and a "right" way of conducting it).[10]

The public seems not always to grasp the many forces and conditions that limit a president's effectiveness. Kennedy once complained, "The powers of the Presidency are often described. Its limitations should occasionally be remembered."[11] Not to appreciate such limitations frequently causes an outpouring of popular criticism not long after a president assumes office. The public quickly sees him as a major cause and not a solution to the nation's problems when he does not immediately become a Samson on either the domestic or the foreign scene. This criticism, often exacerbated by the media, does make the president's job more difficult, as many presidents have maintained.[12]

The public has not been given much opportunity to show its attitude on the standing of past presidents and how well they have surmounted these various difficulties. When it has been asked, however, the results have been disappointing. A Gallup poll in 1956 asking, "What three United States Presidents do you regard as the greater?" had to be aborted because a portion of the 1800 pollees could not correctly name three presidents![13] Another

Gallup poll, also taken in the 1950s, fared somewhat better when it asked a group of people listed in *Who's Who in America* the following question: "From your own personal point of view, which President of the United States would you regard as the greatest?" The results:[14]

President	Percent
Lincoln	45
Washington	19
F. Roosevelt	7
Jefferson	6
Wilson	3
T. Roosevelt	2
Hoover	1
Cleveland	1
Others	1
Don't know	15

A few other public opinion polls have been held, the most recent in 1976, but each of those showed little more than that Lincoln and Washington were always named along with some of the most recent (and therefore known) incumbents as being the best.[15]

Except for Kennedy's comment in connection with the 1962 historians' poll, there has been no reaction by the presidents themselves to the various rankings made by either the public or the scholarly professionals. Yet there is considerable evidence on how recent presidents have felt about their job and the performance of their predecessors in it. Franklin Roosevelt frequently stated that the presidency was preeminently a place of moral leadership. Truman claimed that the president's most important job was "to persuade people to do what they ought to do without having to be persuaded."[16] Eisenhower stated that a president's chief duty was to build and protect national confidence.[17] Whatever their individual views, all recent presidents, like the historians, have shown themselves sympathetic to an activist presidency. Even Eisenhower, Ford, and Carter (and now also Reagan), presidents who tended to downplay the power inherent in the office, considered themselves president "of all the people" and as such were directly responsible for vigorously managing the nation's foreign and domestic policies. All these presidents, whether they succeeded or not, endeavored to give the impression of being "strong" presidents, of promoting new ideas, and of being decisive.

Recent presidents have been outspoken in naming the qualities they believe a good president should possess, and by doing so have provided us with an interesting comparison to the historians' judgments. Of the last nine presidents before Reagan, seven claimed that successful president had to be a skillful politician and that without considerable political experience he would be crippled in handling the job. They further agreed that a successful president had to be intelligent—that is, be quick to grasp situations and be able to assimilate large amounts of information. Lyndon Johnson asserted that toughness and determination were among the prize qualities of a successful president, an assessment with which Richard Nixon also agreed. Truman contended that the greatest qualities needed in a president were high principles and intellectual honesty. Carter stated that what was most needed were integrity of character and inner strength. Other qualities that at one time or another were mentioned by presidents Hoover through Carter were self-restraint, confidence, humaneness, and decisiveness.[18]

Like the historians, presidents too have had their favorites. Although Franklin Roosevelt never pinpointed his choices, he most often referred in his speeches and conversations to Lincoln, and he also admired Woodrow Wilson and Theodore Roosevelt. Truman regarded Franklin Roosevelt himself as one of the truly great presidents of the United States. Truman's other favorites were Lincoln and Wilson. Like Truman, both Kennedy and Lyndon Johnson considered Franklin Roosevelt to be one of the foremost presidents and the one they most wanted to emulate. Although Nixon had the portraits of Wilson and Theodore Roosevelt hung in the Cabinet Room, he once admitted that Lincoln really occupied the first place among the chief executives and that Franklin Roosevelt was not far behind. When Ford entered the White House, he replaced Wilson's and Theodore Roosevelt's pictures in the Cabinet Room with Lincoln's and Truman's, indicating something about his personal feelings in this matter. Carter, in turn, left Truman's portrait there but added a painting of Jefferson. On a number of occasions, Carter also indicated that Franklin Roosevelt belonged in the very front rank of the chief executives. Presidents Reagan and Bush were the only recent presidents to stray somewhat from this pattern. Reagan had Eisenhower's portrait hung over the Cabinet Room mantel, and paintings of Coolidge and Taft placed at the other end of the room.[19] Still, he often indicated his admiration for Franklin Roosevelt and resurrected FDR's ghost from time to time when it suited his purposes.[20]

Such presidential reactions and statements can be taken as confirmation of the views of the professional historians. If one agrees with Kennedy, certainly there are no greater experts on the presidency than the presidents themselves. Yet it would have been surprising if the results of either the public opinion polls or the views of the presidents had been much different from those of the historians with respect to the top presidents in the nation's history. Part of this similarity of opinion is undoubtedly symbiotic, with one group feeding on the conclusions of the others and thereby reenforcing the prevailing result. Some of it certainly stems from popular myth and from certain cultural factors (e.g., Washington's birthday, Lincoln's birthday) that tend to perpetuate universal beliefs but do not illuminate why they are held. But some of it may also spring from an underlying intuitive feeling that in participants and observers alike gives birth to a common concept of what constitutes successful democratic leadership.

Leaving arguments and speculation about such matters aside, we are left with the reality that these few top-rated past presidents provide the examples by which the public, historians, and presidents alike judge other presidential performances. The problem always is to find and elect new presidents who can live up to these examples.

Historians Rank the Presidency of Ronald Reagan: A Test Case of Historical Judgment

THE ORIGINAL PUBLICATION OF THE preceding chapters, presenting the results of the Murray-Blessing Presidential Performance Study, coincided with the final year of the Reagan presidency and the selection of a new president, George Bush, in 1988. In the interest of bringing that study as up-to-date as possible and further testing some of its findings, we launched a new poll soon after the end of the Reagan administration, concentrating solely on Ronald Reagan—his personality, traits, characteristics, and accomplishments as president.

Certainly Reagan provided an excellent test of the Murray-Blessing hypothesis that "outstanding administrative achievements in domestic, foreign, and military affairs emerged as the *sine que non* of presidential greatness." Also, Reagan seemed to be a perfect test for the Murray-Blessing thesis that presidential greatness rests primarily on actual achievement and only secondarily on the character and personality of the person in the Oval Office. After all, only a few presidents have had the looks, the charm, and the affability of Ronald Reagan, and only a few have participated in so many momentous events or proposed such distinctive policies.[1]

As often noted, Reagan is one of the most difficult presidents to understand. He appears to have successfully guarded against revelations about his inner life. It may be impossible to dislike Reagan when one meets him, but it is also virtually impossible to understand him. As his biographer Edmund Morris indicated, no one knows what he actually thinks. Morris has gone so far as to call him the "most mysterious" man he has every met.[2] Reagan's first secretary of state, Alexander Haig, compared the Reagan administration to a "ghost ship":

You heard the creak of the rigging and the groans of the timbers and sometimes even glimpsed the crew on deck. But which of the crew had the helm?[3]

Donald Regan, President Reagan's second chief of staff, spoke about Reagan's having what political scientist Fred Greenstein called the "no-hands" presidency.[4] David Stockman, Reagan's budget chief, reported a presidency and a president constantly adrift.[5] But such observations are tempered by other views. Martin Anderson claimed that Reagan was "a closet workaholic," a view supported by Larry Speakes, his press secretary, and also by Donald Regan.[6] That Reagan was a sound manager who displayed considerable skill has been noted by as unlikely a source as Terrell Bell (who held the unenviable position of secretary of education under Reagan).[7]

The idea that Reagan was controlled and manipulated by his high-powered intimates seems attractive at first, but it may be too simplistic given Reagan's overriding of the opinions of both Secretary of State George Shultz and Secretary of Defense Caspar Weinberger on the administration's dealings with Iran, his angry vetoing of the tax views of Edwin Meese and James Baker, and his rejection of the advice of Michael Deaver (a man who once claimed that he was "Ronald Reagan") concerning President Carter's hostage release agreement with Iran.[8] Moreover, speechwriter Peggy Noonan notwithstanding, there is little reason to believe that Reagan simply mouthed the words of others.[9] Reagan has maintained, and his associates confirm, that up until the time he was actually in office he crafted almost all his own speeches, including the gracious and forward-looking concession speech at the 1976 Republican Convention, his acceptance speech at the 1980 Convention, and his first inaugural speech.[10] One must therefore conclude that Reagan is an extraordinarily complicated man on whom historians and others will probably never agree.

Beginning in late 1988 through early 1990, we wrote, administered, compiled, and analyzed a detailed 164-response nineteen-page survey specifically measuring historians' evaluations of Ronald Reagan (see Appendix 12). Some 750 surveys were sent to American historians chosen at random from the American Historical Association's *Guide to Departments of History for 1986–1987*, the latest edition available at the time of the selection process.[11] Some 481 surveys were completed and returned to us, a return rate of 63 percent. To pre-test some of our questions, we also mailed out

200 copies of a preliminary, much smaller postcard-size survey. A total of 130 were returned, a rate of 65 percent.

Both these polls showed that the reaction of the great majority of American historians to Ronald Reagan has been quite negative, with the mean presidential rating placing him in the Below Average category between Zachary Taylor and John Tyler.[12] To be more precise, given an option between ranking Reagan as Great, Near Great, Above Average, Average, Below Average, or Failure, more than 18 percent of those who answered the long survey declared Reagan a flat failure. Forty-four percent ranked him as Below Average, slightly more than 20 percent rated him as either Above Average of Near Great, and just under 1 percent scored him as Great. The remainder rated his presidency as Average. In short, more than 62 percent of those polled ranked him as Below Average, while only 21 percent rated him Above Average.

The discrepancies in Reagan's rating, which were greater than those for any other president except Nixon, require explanation. As soon as our preliminary postcard poll indicated that there would probably be broad deviations in assessment, we attempted to fine-tune a wide-ranging set of questions for the long survey in hopes of isolating indicators that might show the reasons for such variations. These questions ranged from personal matters (such as the significance of Nancy Reagan) to matters of concrete policy and implementation (such as the bombing of Libya, the stock market crash of 1987, and the nomination of Judge Bork to the Supreme Court). Some questions concerned only general policies ("Was Reagan right in believing [that] the federal government has become dangerously intrusive?"), while others dealt with specific actions ("Did Reagan pursue the correct course in sending ships to patrol the Persian Gulf?").

The long survey explored a multiplicity of potential causes for the rating differences, but it also searched for matters about which historians agreed. The questions eventually were grouped under seven general topics: foreign policy, foreign policy implementation, military affairs, economic affairs, noneconomic domestic affairs, executive policy, and personal characteristics. Although these were artificial divisions, they were set up to make the *survey* as inclusive as possible and yet render the results understandable. Some key items naturally fell outside these divisions ("Would you say that, *in general*, during the Reagan years the morale of the American people improved?") but have been included in the "personal characteristics" category for the light they shed on "intangibles" in the Reagan situation.

Domestic and Social Policies

As we evaluated the different questions and responses, it became readily apparent that the varied reactions of the historians concerning the quality, efficacy, and reasonableness of some of Reagan's actions were at least partially the result of fundamental socioeconomic divisions within the American historical profession itself. For example, during the Reagan years the American economy underwent one of the longest and largest expansions in American history. The gross national product rose by 80 percent, inflation dropped by 10 percent (from a little more than 13 percent per annum during the last year of the Carter administration), and the unemployment rate fell to nearly 5 percent in Reagan's last years.[13]

Yet more than 35 percent of the historians polled believed that Reagan deserved little credit for this advance, and only 17 percent believed he should receive a good deal of credit for it. Historians overwhelmingly condemned the tax cuts of 1981 and the tax reform of 1986. Indeed, most historians (89 percent) believed that upper socioeconomic groups were undertaxed even *before* the tax cuts of 1981. A somewhat smaller but still substantial majority (66 percent) believed that the economic advance was confined only to the top sectors of American society. In addition, 58 percent blamed the Reagan forces squarely for bringing on the 1981–1982 recession; 56 percent believed that Reagan's policies "contributed greatly" to the stock crash of 1987; 70 percent saw the president as being more to blame for the budget deficit than Congress; and slightly more than 66 percent held that the president was more responsible for the trade deficit than Congress. In short, it appears that the majority of historians do not believe that Reagan can claim credit for the economic advances of the 1980s, and a substantial number would redefine the meaning of the term "economic advance" as applied to the Reagan years.

On matters of social policy, Reagan fared even worse at the hands of the survey historians than he did on economic policy. Indeed, it would not be wrong to conclude that the broad majority of those polled regarded Reagan's social policy as both wrong-headed and malignant. For instance, 66 percent of the respondents described Reagan as either very racist or somewhat racist, while another 19 percent regarded him as "mildly racist." In terms of gender, 33 percent held Reagan to be very sexist, 40 percent regarded him as being somewhat sexist, and only eleven percent classified him as being evenhanded. It is clear that—despite Reagan's own statements on the subject of discrimination, his appointment of the first woman Supreme Court Justice and the first black national security advisor, and his mix of gender and race in high-ranking positions—American historians felt that the underlying thrust of the Reagan administration was against equal rights and equal access.[14]

Reagan's appointees, such as Supreme Court Justice Sandra O'Connor, did not help Reagan in any concrete way. On a scale of 1 (Excellent) to 6 (Poor), O'Connor, whom Reagan called "everything I hoped for," had a below-average rating of 3.27 among the polled historians.[15] Reagan's other Supreme Court appointments fared no better. Justice Arthur Kennedy received a 3.8 rating on the same scale, Justice Anthony Scalia received a 3.9 rating, and the appointment of Justice William Rehnquist as Chief Justice received a subterranean 4.1. Moreover, just as the historians downgraded Reagan's justices, so too did they downgrade Reagan's views of the judicial process. The nomination of Judge Robert Bork was disapproved by more than three-quarters of the respondents. It is indicative of the apparently substantive disagreements between the survey historians who supported Reagan and those who did not that 57 percent said Judge Bork was well qualified for the Supreme Court in terms of judicial and legal expertise but should not have been seated anyway. In short, for a majority of the historians, Bork's judicial and legal expertise, although accepted, was not sufficient to overcome Bork's views on issues of substance.

Two other questions illuminated some of the differences over substantive judicial issues. When asked about Reagan's desire to have the courts apply a stricter construction to the Constitution, only slightly more than 20 percent of the historians approved of Reagan's stand, while 57 percent strongly disapproved. When asked to evaluate Reagan on a more specific (and gender-related) issue, more than 77 percent of the responding historians believed Reagan was wrong in his views on *Roe v. Wade*. Thus, with respect to Supreme Court appointments, the pursuit of racial and gender equality, and Reagan's view of the law and the judicial process—three closely interrelated matters—most American historians strongly disagreed with Reagan.

With regard to other domestic activities, the survey historians soundly condemned Reagan. Some 88 percent believed that welfare and social programs were underfunded during the Reagan years. In particular, most respondents held that Medicare, student loans, women's programs, aid to secondary education, and aid to minorities (including set-asides) were all undersupported. Sixty-five percent believed that Reagan should bear a great deal of the blame for *creating* a body of homeless in the United States, and nearly 82 percent claimed that the Reagan administration should have done much more to help such unfortunates. It is not too surprising that 77 percent of all the responding historians believed the Reagan forces should have spent more on public housing. The majority, though, agreed with Reagan that existing public-housing programs had been generally unsuccessful.

In terms of domestic affairs, both economic and social, the overwhelming majority of the survey historians disapproved of the Reagan domestic policies. Reagan stands accused of racism, sexism, flawed judicial policies, underfunding of social and domestic programs, and creating and ignoring the homeless—a range of accusations to rival those leveled at any other president's domestic program. Indeed, one respondent attached to his questionnaire a clipping from the book *By the Few for the Few*, written by two members of the Center for the Study of Social Policy and endorsed by Hale Champion, executive dean of the John F. Kennedy School of Government at Harvard.[16] The clipping reads in part:

> President Reagan's policies reflect the philosophy that government bears little or no responsibility for disadvantaged citizens. This philosophy is certainly evident in the case of working-poor female headed families . . . . Poor households have had to do with less. Many students are in jeopardy of no longer qualifying for student loans. Farmers are witnessing the foreclosing of farms because farm price supports have lapsed. Victims of discrimination due to race, disability, or gender have found the administration deaf to their pleas. Hundreds of thousands of physically and mentally disturbed adults have had their Social Security disability benefits terminated. . . . All of these groups are casualties.[17]

Reagan's domestic actions received support, or at least escaped majority condemnation, on only three counts. Reagan was not blamed for the American farm crisis of the 1980s (only 23 percent of respondents agreed that the farmers' problems were "*more* the result of the Reagan administration's handling of the problem"); his calls for long prison terms for drug kingpins were strongly backed (slightly more than 82 percent approved); and his proposals for stiff prison terms for violent and habitual criminals also received firm support (almost 76 percent approved).

Foreign Policy and Foreign-Policy Implementation

With respect to foreign policy, the judgment of the historians was more mixed, although the respondents still condemned much of the Reagan record. For instance, 63 percent of historians characterized Reagan's bombing of Libya as both unlawful *and* contrary to the nation's best interests. They soundly criticized Reagan for believing that the stability of the South African government was more important to the United States than South Africa's internal and racial policies. Almost 81 percent claimed that it was not in America's best interests to invade Grenada. Sixty-one percent believed that Reagan's shipment of arms to the Afghans had either a limited effect or no effect at all on the Soviet withdrawal. Some 78 percent stated that Reagan was too tolerant of Israel's occasional military incursions against its neighbors. And almost 75 percent sharply downgraded Reagan's dealings with El Salvador, while nearly the same percentage disapproved of his relations with Mexico.

Concerning the present drift toward more representative government around the world, Reagan received slightly better, if qualified, ratings. In the South Korean passage from military rule to a more democratic government, 40 percent of the historians believed the Reagan administration steered a prudent course, almost 37 percent claimed that it gave too little help to the forces of democracy, and more than 20 percent stated that the United States should have stayed out of the Korean situation altogether. Some 64 percent give Reagan good marks for facilitating the transfer of power from Marcos to Aquino in the Philippines, and an even larger group—well over three-quarters of all respondents—credited Reagan for his support of the Aquino regime after the Marcos ouster. Almost the same division of opinion indicated that the Reagan administration had played too much of a role in *keeping* Marcos in power.

American historians split almost evenly over Reagan's impact on the emergence of a nonaligned Eastern Europe. For example, slightly more than 54 percent concluded that Reagan's level of support for Solidarity was appropriate for the situation. In the promotion of a more democratic government in Chile, opinion on Reagan's policy was divided: 52 percent blamed Reagan for his lack of action, and almost 37 percent blamed him for too much action regarding that country. No such ambivalence existed regarding Reagan and Nicaragua. Those polled (73 percent) rejected the idea that the

Sandinistas were a serious threat to the stability of Central America, and by wide margins (88 percent to 12 percent) they condemned the Reagan administration's support for the Contras (even with the Iran-Contra affair excluded).[18]

Regarding Iran-Contra, the response of the historians can easily be summarized—the survey historians did not believe Reagan's protestations of innocence. More than 76 percent claimed that Reagan knew he was actually swapping arms for hostages, and almost 85 percent stated that Reagan was also aware Iranian money was flowing into the coffers of the Contras. Regardless of whether these historians are right, the perception of shifty dealings by such an overwhelming number inevitably has affected Reagan's presidential reputation.[19]

The survey historians were not as negative about Reagan's Middle Eastern policy, but few considered it an outright success. Although large majorities (84 percent and 91 percent) believed that Reagan was right in trying to open lines of communication with Iranian leaders and with the Palestine Liberation Organization, a majority also held that the actual execution of his Mideast policy reflected "a record of ineptitude." With regard to handling terrorism, 54 percent of the responding historians scored the Reagan record as very poor, while 82 percent rated it below average. The survey historians likewise indicated that the Reagan confrontations with Libya did not reflect positively on the administration, with almost 50 percent suggesting that both sides were "about equally" at fault. Almost 10 percent placed the blame squarely on the United States. Nearly 70 percent of responding historians dismissed Reagan's attempts to impose order in Beirut as "not a good idea." In the Persian Gulf, however, Reagan's policies received the majority support of the historians. By and large, they backed the Reagan military initiative there by 65 percent, although one-third of those who supported Reagan felt that the United States seemed to be too ready to commit to action in the Gulf. (All surveys were completed before the Persian Gulf crisis and war.)

The relationship between Reagan and the Soviet Union evoked a more positive response. Although slightly more than 50 percent of the respondents believed the Reagan-Gorbachev meetings (with the exception of Reykjavik) were "really too mixed to assess," 42 percent stated that the summits were a credit to Reagan.[20] The Reagan administration received praise for the INF treaty (78 percent rated his performance between 1 and 3 on a scale of 1 to 6 on this answer), and 56 percent believed that, in general, the Reagan forces handled negotiations with the Soviets well. On the other hand, despite the majority praise for those negotiations, most of the historians (71 percent) believed that Reagan distrusted the Soviets too much. In the light of such response, it is not surprising that most historians believed he was too timid in finally encouraging *glasnost* and *perestroika*. Although more than 50 percent approved this latter course, a substantial 26 percent wished Reagan had pushed earlier and more vigorously for reform within the Soviet Union. In this connection, 69 percent concluded either that Reagan followed a prudent course in pushing for human rights in the Soviet Union or that he should have "pushed even harder" for the Soviets to move forward on human rights.

Military Affairs and Intangibles

While American historians were slightly more positive on Reagan's foreign policy and actions than on his domestic affairs, they certainly did not believe that his military policy (except in the Persian Gulf) was either correct or effective. The Strategic Defense Initiative (Star Wars) was considered a "bad idea" in terms of costs, strategic implications, and/or practicality by 82 percent of the historians. A substantial 45 percent saw the general military buildup as being too much; only slightly more than 10 percent saw it as either about right or too little, while almost twice that number (20 percent) regarded it as totally unnecessary. It is interesting that the recurrent flaps over military procurement did not seem to have had much influence on these judgments. When asked "If the weapons and supplies used by the armed services could be secured more efficiently than they are now, would you have the same feelings about a military buildup?" more than 95 percent said they would retain the same opinions.

Those polled also claimed that the military buildup had little influence on a change in the Soviet Union's military posture, with only 10 percent believing that it played a key role in *any* Soviet change. Indeed, a majority (52 percent) asserted that the buildup played only a minor role or no role at all in prompting Soviet changes. This position of the American historians seems to suggest that their relatively favorable view of Reagan's Soviet policies rested largely on his administration's ability to take advantage of situations rather than causing or creating new departures.[21]

Turning to Reagan's personal conduct of the presidential office, one is struck by several salient and conflicting judgments. Some 92 percent of the responding historians considered Reagan unqualified for the presidency in terms of intellect, and 54 percent believed he was unqualified in terms of

both intellect *and* experience. In addition, these historians judged his administration to have been among the most corrupt in American history. His
personal integrity was assessed as either average or below average by 84.5
percent of respondents. His impact on the nation's value system was thought
by 68 percent of the historians to have been significant but negative, and
insignificant by 18 percent. Almost 81 percent agreed that he left behind
only a small-to-moderate legislative legacy, and 70 percent said he was only
a weak-to-moderate party leader. Finally, a crushing 92 percent of respondents believed that the American people "have overestimated Mr. Reagan."

Yet, as with so many judgments concerning Reagan's record, there is
a certain ambivalence. Most (84 percent) dismissed the notion that Reagan
was driven blindly by his conservative ideals, with more than 64 percent
stating that he was an expert blender of idealism and pragmatism. Almost
20 percent characterized him as primarily a pragmatist. More than 64 percent
claimed that *"over the long haul . . .* presidents in general" would be better
off adopting Reagan's style of delegation of authority rather than the Carter
style of personal involvement in the details of governmental management.
Furthermore, these historians ranked Reagan high in terms of charismatic
leadership, with 69 percent giving him either a very high or high rating in
the art of "getting people to follow him where he wanted to go." Almost
80 percent of those polled believed that the morale of the American people
improved during the Reagan years, and the great majority of that 80 percent
attributed much of this improvement to Reagan himself. Finally, the survey
historians by a wide margin (74 percent to 26 percent) believed that under
Ronald Reagan the office of the presidency became stronger (more than one-
third said much stronger) than it had been under recent previous presidents.

Although space limited the number of tangential questions that could
be asked, it is clear that the historians believed that Reagan should have
held more news conferences, that he was too loyal to his subordinates, and
that he showed poor judgment in allowing Nancy Reagan (whom 78 percent
of historians ranked either negatively or very negatively) to have as much
influence as she did. Reagan was also faulted for being "too attentive" to
the "Moral Right," and he was thought to have been aware of CIA Director
William Casey's illegal attempts to remove the CIA from congressional
oversight. In short, even though his *style* of management was preferred to
Carter's, his actual conduct of the office was still persistently downgraded.

Given the general rejection by the survey historians of the Reagan
administration and its policies and their criticism of Reagan's intelligence,
integrity, and judgment, there seems to be little chance that Reagan's his-

torical reputation can be markedly upgraded. Indeed, because the historians endorsed Reagan's abilities and actions only in reference to matters of impression and style, and gave him qualified support only in the area of Soviet relations and the spread of democracy, there seem to be no grounds on which a more favorable revision of Reagan's place in history can be based.

In reality, though, there are some reasons to suspect that Reagan's rating may not remain where it currently is. In this present survey, a favorable minority view of Reagan came from a sizable group of scholars who consistently read the Reagan record differently from the majority. This minority group repeatedly ranked Reagan higher on almost all issues, with foreign-policy ratings somewhat higher than the domestic and economic policy ratings. Overall, this group, which comprised as much as 25 percent of the responding historians, ranked Reagan in the Above Average category with a few Near Great rankings added. Using Guttman Scaling to divide the survey's answers into positive and negative ratings and to create separate scores for economic policy, domestic noneconomic policy, foreign policy, foreign-policy implementation, military policy, intangibles, and personal characteristics, the correlations between overall ranking and individual scales indicated that the relationship between the perception of performance and the perception of greatness (or lack thereof) was very high.[22] On the other hand, the correlations between ranking and intangibles (such as leadership) or personal characteristics (such as honesty) were much less strong, reflecting the fact that there were only a few consistent associations between personal characteristics and eventual ratings.

At the end of each survey questionnaire, the respondents were asked to sum up Reagan the president in four adjectives or adjective phrases, and then to sum up Reagan the person in four adjectives or adjective phrases. It was not uncommon to find those who ranked Reagan Above Average making such remarks as "often misguided," "fiscally irresponsible," "rather unintelligent," "out of touch," and so on. At the same time, many who ranked Reagan low saw him as being "forceful," "sincere," "strong," and even "possessing great personal gifts" (this last from a historian who ranked Reagan a failure).

In brief, in assessing Reagan's success, historians tended to separate Reagan the individual—and even Reagan the individual as president— rather sharply from the policies of the Reagan administration. Nevertheless, in the final analysis, the historians' rating rested mainly on whether the Reagan policies had worked. Had the Reagan whom many historians pictured as excelling in charismatic leadership led the nation to results they could honestly applaud, some of Reagan's other personal characteristics (e.g., to whom he was married, who his friends were) would probably have mattered little.

It could be argued that to some extent Reagan's accomplishments were prejudged, that an academic bias against his conservative philosophy and a distaste for what many perceived as Reagan's simplistic approach to issues predetermined the low rating outcome. Some liberal bias undoubtedly did exist, and conservative-oriented scholars also probably were swayed to some extent in their answers by their own predilections. Nonetheless, we were powerfully struck by a statement appended to one survey response that judged Reagan a failure:

> I hate to appear to be so biased against Reagan . . . but you asked for an honest opinion. I am not necessarily a "New Left" historian, but I do have a low opinion of U.S. foreign policy and domestic policy when it comes to civil rights, liberties, etc. I am frustrated but continue to try and be professional in the classroom. I emphasize historiography in all my courses, hoping to at least expose my students to all viewpoints.

After reading and analyzing the returns of all the respondents, the conclusion was inescapable that the vast majority of historians did not take the ranking of Reagan lightly and that they responded to the survey in a most serious and professional manner.

It still seems likely that Reagan's ranking, as with that of all previous presidents, will ultimately rest on the strength of his accomplishments. Thus, if the current historical judgment of Reagan's accomplishments changes, his ranking will undoubtedly rise. A comparison of all the various presidential polls has indicated that a president's ranking is at its lowest shortly after his leaving office and that it requires about a generation (25 to 30 years) for his place in the rankings to achieve a stable resting place. In this connection, the Reagan survey revealed some grounds on which a Reagan revisionism could be based. He did change the structure of taxation in a number of significant ways. He did have an impact on the now-defunct Soviet Union that may have affected its demise. He did promote a military buildup that his successor used to advantage in Panama and in the Persian Gulf War. His views on domestic policy, while not always translated into legislation, dominated American discourse on the subject for well over a decade, and his impact on the economic well-being of the nation during his tenure was significant, although its efficacy will be debated for a long time. Likewise, his effect on the judiciary was undeniable, but again the results remain debatable. Finally, Reagan's ability to persuade, his ability to motivate, and his style in manipulating late-twentieth-century American politics is reminiscent of Franklin Roosevelt, especially in the latter's use of the media in the 1930s and 1940s.

The debate over Reagan and the Reagan inheritance will unquestionably be a long and lively one. The present survey defines the main issues on which an assessment of Reagan will largely depend. Furthermore, whatever the eventual outcome and whenever a historical consensus is reached, the survey indicates that Reagan's presidential reputation will ultimately rest on the measured judgments of historians reacting to substantive fact. The survey has taken only a snapshot of a possible historical verdict at a very early point in the ultimate evaluation process, but it is one that may serve as an important benchmark for later comparisons.

Conclusions

AMONG POLITICAL SCIENTISTS and other scholarly observers of the presidency, there has recently been a quest to find reliable predictors for a successful performance in the White House. Quantitative analyses of personality traits and the construction of presidential models have encouraged a belief that the difficult task of selecting proper presidential leadership can be simplified and reduced to a workable formula. The ultimate hope is that a "potentially great" president can be picked out of the crowd even before he is elected.

All the studies thus far have led to no such achievement. The best they can do is help us delineate more accurately what has been, but they have not yet enabled us to select what is to be. Using the rankings of the presidents in the various historian polls since 1948, one study has estimated that approximately 75 percent of the variance in presidential greatness can be accounted for by such factors as administration duration, number of war years, administration scandals, time of party control of Congress, number of acts passed by Congress, number of treaties negotiated, and so on.[1] Another study has maintained that as much as 84 percent of the variance in presidential success can be explained by combining the differences in presidential activeness and decisiveness with those in administration accomplishments.[2] Maybe so. But all such details about a president and his administration are known only *after* he has been elected and served.

One recent intriguing theory, advanced by political science professor James David Barber of Duke, contends that there is a recurrent rhythm in American politics and that this rhythm has three themes: politics as conflict, politics as conscience, and politics as conciliation. Professor Barber claims that this sequence runs its course over a period of twelve years and then repeats itself: there is first a battle for power (the elections of 1900, 1912, 1924, 1936, 1948, 1960, and 1972), then a revival of social conscience and moral verities (1904, 1916, 1928, 1940, 1952, 1964, and 1976), and finally the emergence of a "politics of joy" (1908, 1920, 1932, 1944, 1956, 1968, and 1980). Although admitting that such historical patterning oversimplifies, Barber nonetheless contends that this rhythm not only exists but also presages the kind of presidential leadership we will get in any one of the twelve-year periods.[3]

Another of Professor Barber's theories, first appearing in his *The Presidential Character* (1972), which carried the provocative subtitle "Predicting Performance in the White House," claims that there have been four presidential personality types in the nation's history: (1) active-positive (they want to achieve results); (2) active-negative (they aim to get and keep power); (3) passive-positive (they want to be revered); and (4) passive-negative (they emphasize civic virtue). As examples of these types, he mentions Franklin Roosevelt, Truman, Kennedy, and Jefferson as active-positive; Wilson, Hoover, Lyndon Johnson, and Nixon as active-negative; Harding, Madison, and Taft as passive-positive; and Washington, Coolidge, and Eisenhower as passive-negative.[4]

At issue here is not whether these theories of Professor Barber are valid or whether such patterning distorts the historical record beyond credulity. The point is that such theories do not help us predict the *quality* of presidential leadership regardless of the personality type or the time period involved. The Murray-Blessing historians found high-ranked and low-ranked chief executives in all of the above rhythmic periods and (except for the active-positive group, which Barber prefers) in each of the personality types.

Because the presidency is both an institution and an individual, historians have long suspected that no such categorization of the office, regardless of how carefully constructed, is likely to ring true for all times and all situations. Because the presidency is to a large extent what the president thinks it is, who and what he is, even more than the office's institutional structure, finally determines its actual parameters. As Woodrow Wilson wrote long before he assumed the position, "The President's office is anything he has the sagacity and force to make it."[5] Ever unpredictable and changing, this personal aspect of the presidency renders futile any attempt to define it fully or to prejudge greatness in it with any degree of accuracy.

Each president in history has been special and, as Lyndon Johnson liked to say, "We have only one of them at a time."[6] The presidency is held not only by one person at a time but also at a given moment in time. Time, so important to the historian, is never the same and is ever moving onward. This adds a most confusing dimension to the presidential office. The specific circumstances, economic conditions, foreign crises, technological and scientific challenges, and changing public attitudes that confront each successive president make prognostications impossible. More than this, no one can foretell the *subsequent* flow of historical events that will also influence a president's ultimate standing.

Both presidents and professional president-watchers cannot escape the fact that "time" does hold a president hostage in two important ways. First, most of the problems a president encounters will have been shaped for him by the impersonal forces of the past. Whatever his ability and energy, he will be able to alter them only in a modest way during his brief tenure. Second, the day a president leaves office his place in history depends to some degree on the history that has not been written yet. Theodore Roosevelt knew this, once observing that although he had pursued his policies because he thought they were right, only the future would decide the correctness of his actions. "I hope that time will justify them," he commented, "[but] if it does not, why, I must abide the fall of the dice."[7]

Along with all the other attributes, the survey historians felt that a truly successful president had to possess a "sense of history." Almost all presidents have claimed that in the long run history would vindicate their policies. No president who ever lost the office failed to express confidence that history would rate his presidency more highly than the electorate did. Nixon, Ford, and Carter were merely the last in a long line of chief executives to maintain that.

Having a sense of history, however, is something quite different from this. It involves the ability to separate the transient from the permanent, the secondary from the primary—to see the subtle connections between causes and effects. It includes the ability to grasp the whole in its proper proportion, to discover the generating principle that is shaping the future because of the trend of things currently in motion. It means shunning short-term political successes that can be easily won today in order to tackle the more serious and controversial problems that may prevent tomorrow's ruin. All the Great and Near Great presidents had this ability; the lower-ranked presidents did not.[8]

Subsequent history and the passage of time also have a "purging" affect on the contemporary record, which in turn can drastically effect a president's historic rating. As the survey historians correctly maintained, television, the press, popular opinion, and White House public relations may help elect or defeat a president, but they do not supply an adequate basis for historical judgment.[9] Only the passage of time provides the framework necessary to separate the false from the real by transferring a president and his administration from the present to the past, where sober reflection, comparisons, and contrasts can reign.

If the nation's chief executives have been hostages of subsequent history, they also have been captives of the presidency itself. Not one of them failed to be deeply affected by the office, and all quickly discovered that their impact on the presidency was often less than the presidency's impact on them. Many a man thought to be common seemingly became quite uncommon once in the presidential chair. This is yet another factor subtly influencing presidential performance that cannot be predicted or fully explained. The presidency has tended to bring out the best qualities in most incumbents, forcing them into a kind of overdrive and making them reach beyond their normal capabilities.[10]

Judging from the results of past presidential polls, the various yardsticks used by the Murray-Blessing historians to gauge presidential performances were much the same as those used by the evaluators before them. Yet there are some president-watchers who claim that a change in evaluating the presidency is currently taking place. This contention rests on an assumption that Americans are in transit from a Ptolemaic to a Copernican view of themselves and their nation's power. The resultant scaling down of national ambition, it is claimed, will inevitably bruise many old myths—among them, what constitutes greatness in the White House. According to this view, the standard example of the active, aggressive presidency is no longer valid. Such a presidency, they say, is too moralistic, makes for a passive citizenry, creates cynicism when things go awry, and encourages the incumbent to attempt more than he can deliver.[11]

These presidential observers now see virtue in an eight-year presidency in which nothing really bad takes place and no time bombs are left for the future. Eisenhower's recent elevation in ranking by the historians is used as evidence of this changing attitude. Professor Fred Greenstein, professor of politics and law at Princeton, was among the critics in the 1950s who dismissed Eisenhower as a lightweight, only to write a book in 1982 lauding him. According to Professor Greenstein, Eisenhower rescued us from the prevailing view that the presidency is, or ought to be, "a vehicle for 100-day explosions of activity, or for steely showdowns in crisis periods."[12]

Whatever may be happening to the thinking of some presidential observers, there is as yet no firm indication that a similar development is occurring among rank-and-file historians. If the Murray-Blessing respondents are to be believed, an effective president may come from almost any profession or any political background. He may possess any appearance, be almost any age, and have almost any kind of education. He may be born in any region of the country, be religious or nonreligious, and married or unmarried. But to be truly successful, he must act boldly and decisively and show intelligence, vision, courage, and determination. Such a president must be a skillful manipulator of people, have the ability to communicate and inspire, and be a crafty politician. He need not disclose everything to the public, but he must possess integrity and a workable ethic that promotes the general welfare and rises above mere expediency.

Great presidents, in turn, are associated with grave crises or major developments in the nation's history. According to the survey historians, they do not merely survive these challenges but leave an indelible mark on the nation through the outstanding accomplishments of their administrations. Such accomplishments are not directed at conserving the status quo but are devoted to expanding the external power of the United States and to broadening and strengthening the economic, social, political, and cultural opportunities of the American people. In short, a vigorous, active presidency that combines "the times," personality traits, strength of character, and administration accomplishments into a balanced whole still possesses the most valid claim to true greatness.

We cannot be sure, but we anticipate that the views of these historians are not likely to alter much even in the face of possible changes in the type of persons who hold the presidency. The day is approaching when the English-Irish-Scotch-German monopoly on presidential backgrounds will end and a Jew, a Hawaiian, a Polish-, Italian-, Greek-, or Spanish-American may be elected as chief executive. Also, the day may arrive when a woman or an African-American will be president. It is significant that almost 60 percent of the survey historians accepted the idea of a female president and believed that she could work effectively within the American governmental system. They also believed (76 to 24 percent) that a white female would probably be more acceptable to the electorate than an African-American male.[13] In any case, whoever might hold the office of president in the foreseeable future—he or she, black or white—will probably be subject to the same criteria for greatness as all previous presidents.

Almost a century ago, Lord Bryce wrote in his *American Commonwealth* that great men do not become president in the United States because "the ordinary American voter does not object to mediocrity." Influenced by the generally poor quality of presidents from Jackson to Cleveland, Bryce further claimed that in America great men usually succumbed to the lure of business or entered other pursuits and only rarely went into politics. Even when they did, Bryce contended, the American method of selecting presidents did not bring them to the top.[14]

Lord Bryce was but one of many critics of the presidency who have dotted the nation's history, always claiming that the office is defective and should be changed. Not long ago, George Reedy, a special assistant to Lyndon Johnson felt so despondent about the situation that he published a book entitled *The Twilight of the Presidency*, in which he maintained that the office had outlived its usefulness.[15] Professor Harold M. Barger has elaborated on this pessimistic theme by stating, "The fitting catchword for [the presidency] today might well be the *impossible presidency*." He goes on to claim that however well the office may once have worked, it has now "grown impossible because of important changes in American life and because of dramatic alterations in the political and economic balance globally." As a consequence of such changes, concludes Barger, the presidency has become more and more discredited, and this in turn has given rise to "the phenomenon of disposable presidents."[16] In an atmosphere of such doomsaying, concrete proposals for change have abounded, ranging all the way from creating a president and three assistant presidents to having dual presidents to shoulder the presidential burden. The public itself has often displayed a crisis mentality with respect to the presidency, experiencing a recurrent horror that all is not well with the office.

Defects in the presidential system do exist, not the least of which has been the tendency to select presidents on the basis of their availability rather than on their ability to lead. As we have seen, many of the qualities that make for a good presidential candidate or that contribute to his electability (physical appearance, educational and geographic background, religious belief, marital fidelity, and so on) have had little or nothing to do with ensuring success in the White House. Still, the selection system has worked better than the critics have claimed, and better than we sometimes suspect.

The thirty-nine individuals, including Reagan, who have held the office have actually been a highly select group. One myth of the presidency holds that many of these were "common" men, but in reality they were not. Not even our failing presidents were common men in the commonly accepted sense of the term. Certainly no one has gained the presidency by living a common experience. Luck may have played a part in the rise of some to the

White House, but no average person would have survived the drastic winnowing process along the way. Serving first in another high political capacity, or achieving success in some other field, such as the military, the presidents were in a relatively elite group to begin with. Required in the nation's early years to run the gauntlet of state and party caucuses or conventions, their final selection was not as haphazard as it sometimes seemed. In more recent times, the grueling experience of the presidential primaries, capped by the national nominating conventions, the election campaigns, and presidential debates, has hardly resulted in a "common" man reaching the White House. As unstructured and random as this selection process has been, presidential races throughout the nation's history have resulted in a kind of political survival-of-the-fittest, the overall success of which the rankings of the survey historians have confirmed.

Also, the American public has not been as interested in mediocrity, as easily duped, or as undiscriminating in its presidential voting as Lord Bryce and others have feared. Not a single president ranked Great or Near Great by the historians failed to gain reelection at the hands of the electorate. One, classified as Great, was reelected three times. There is no telling the number of terms Washington might have held had he wanted, or Jefferson or Jackson for that matter. In eras when lower-ranked presidents were in the majority (the immediate pre–Civil War and post–Civil War periods), none managed to hold on to the White House for more than one term, except for Lincoln and Grant. Also, except for those two, Cleveland was the only president from 1833 to 1893 to be given two terms by the voting public. Similarly, in the post–World War II era, the presidents ranked low by the historians failed to be reendorsed by the American people, except for Nixon and Reagan. This suggests that the public has generally been its own best judge of presidential success or failure. [17]

The years 1988 and 1989 marked the 200th anniversary of the office of president—one of the longest-running continuous elective posts in human history. During these two centuries, the change in the American nation has been phenomenal. From a struggling country of 4 million persons in thirteen eastern seaboard states, it has grown to 250 million in fifty states, spreading from the Atlantic Coast to the Pacific Ocean. Its boundaries contain every race and every creed, representing the largest melting pot the world has ever seen. An agricultural nation to begin with, the United States has become the leading industrial, technological, and military nation in the world. Often ignored in its infancy by the nations of that day, it is presently not merely the leader of the Western world, but no nation, no matter where it exists, can chart its course without considering the reactions of the United States. The American presidency, in turn, has paralleled this development exactly. The holder of that office is currently the single most visible political figure in the world and is the custodian of power that no Caesar or Alexander could have dreamed of.

The early presidents would undoubtedly rub their eyes in amazement at this transformation and perhaps feel unequal to shoulder the burdens of the presidency again. Yet throughout the nation's history, men have done so, and the story of that custodianship is still unfolding. The historical record has shown that the presidency has been flexible enough to meet changing conditions and to provide the qualities of leadership required to match contemporary needs. Even critics who have despaired over the caliber of the modern presidency can take heart. Of the last nine presidents (since 1933, including Reagan), five have been judged by the historians to be Great, Near Great, or Above Average. Only one has been dubbed a failure. The fact that two of these men were originally elected only as vice-president and that one wasn't even elected to the vice-presidency before becoming president should also partially allay fears about the presidential selection process. Only the first six presidents (Washington through John Q. Adams) had a higher average ranking than the eight from Franklin Roosevelt through Carter, making the modern era of the presidency in the eyes of professional historians the second most successful in history.[18]

In 1788, Alexander Hamilton predicted that "the office of President will never fall to the lot of any man who is not in an eminent degree endowed with the requisite qualifications. . . . There will be a constant probability of seeing the station filled by characters preeminent for ability and virtue."[19] This was perhaps too sanguine a prediction. Yet the record of the 39 past presidents (Washington through Reagan) generally confirms Hamilton's contention and shows that we have been uncommonly fortunate in the presidential leadership we have enjoyed. The fact that eight of these men (more than one out of five) could be judged Great or Near Great is comforting. When the other nine who were named as Above Average are added to this list, the probability of having a successful performance in the White House rises even higher. Any business organization, university, or foundation, with a much more controlled selection process, would be delighted with such a track record on the part of its chief executives.

American historians as a group are optimistic, if one can judge by their responses to the Murray-Blessing survey. Perhaps the overall success of the American democratic experience has made them that way. In any event, although they too agreed at the outset that the presidency is an immeasurable and impossible job, they showed this not to be true in the case of the men who have held it. During the dark days of Watergate, one professional president-watcher asked, "How can the presidency be made safe for democracy?"[20] The resounding answer by these historians is that the presidency *has* been safe for democracy and will probably continue to be so.

Appendixes

Appendix 1

Survey Pamphlet
for
The Presidential Performance Study

© 1981

(814) 865-1367

November 15, 1981

Dear Colleague:

   As explained in my original contact letter in October, this survey instrument is being sent to you as well as to other PhD's teaching fulltime in American history. The questions are the result of consultations with and suggestions from a large number of you and have been field-tested over the past six months. They have been specifically designed to have a cross-reference relationship to each other and to pinpoint attitudes which, when analyzed by computer, will reveal much about the thinking of historians on the presidency. Each question has been inserted because of its usefullness even though it may at first appear to be frivolous, impertinent, or even irrelevant.

   Our instructions to you are simple. First, do not be deterred by the size of the pamphlet. No one historian will take the whole survey; rather, instructions are provided throughout the survey directing you to differing pages depending on your area of specialty. Second, answer strictly for yourself. There are not a large number of American historians and every voice counts. For instance, if we ask you if some action or idea is acceptable, we are interested in whether that action or idea is acceptable to you. Finally, read the instructions for the questions carefully and then when finished slip the pamphlet into the prepaid envelope and return it to us as soon as convenient.

   A number of personal oral interviews of non-respondents will be conducted by members of our staff in the Winter and Spring of 1982. As indicated in our October letter, the findings will eventually be published. It should be emphasized, however, that all replies are confidential and no attribution of answers to any individual will be made. The basic personal data asked for on the survey will be used only in a collective manner. It will be machine-coded and grouped for the sole purpose of interpreting the data.

   I hope that this experience will not be entirely unpleasant for you and may even serve to sharpen your own thoughts on what constitutes a satisfactory presidential performance. We thank you again for your cooperation; this study cannot succeed without your willing participation.

                                        Sincerely yours,

                                        Robert K. Murray
                                        Director and Professor
                                        of American History

PAGE 2

Section I
Part A
(to be completed by historians only -- non-historians go to Section I, Part B)

1. Year of birth: 19__;   2. Male__; Female__;
3. State where born_____;
4. Education above high school:
   College or University   State   Degree and Year

   _____   _____   _____
   _____   _____   _____
   _____   _____   _____

5. Name of PhD mentor (dissertation supervisor) _____
6. Major area and period of teaching and/or research
specialty (check only one in Column A and only one in Column
B)

        COLUMN A   COLUMN B (cont.)
____ Colonial and Revolutionary   ____ Women's History
____ National Period   ____ U.S. Military
____ Middle Period   ____ U.S. Political
____ Civil War and Reconstruction   ____ U.S. Cultural and Social
____ U.S. 1877-1900   ____ U.S. Diplomatic
____ U.S. 1900-1945   ____ U.S. Economic
____ U.S. since 1945   ____ U.S. Intellectual
                                    ____ U.S. Legal and Constitutional
        COLUMN B   ____ Southern
____ Urban and Quantitative   ____ Western and Frontier
____ Afro-American   ____ State and Local
____ American Indian   ____ Immigration and Ethnic
                                    ____ Other(specify)_____
7. Number of undergraduate students taught in an average year:_____
8. Number of graduate students taught in an average year:_____
9. Total number of PhD's supervised (chief mentor):_____
10. Total number of publications:
   Edited Books: Joint-Authored   Monographs or   Refereed   Others
                    Books   Single-Authored Books Articles
   _____ _____   _____ _____ _____

****
Section I
Part B
(to be completed by non-historians only)
1. Year of Birth 19__;   2. State where born _____;
3. Education above high school:
   College or University   State   Degree and Year

   _____   _____   _____
   _____   _____   _____
   _____   _____   _____

4. Occupation (check primary function)
      ____ Syndicated columnist   ____ TV journalist
      ____ Academician   ____ Newspaper journalist
      ____ Newspaper or magazine editor ____ Politician
      ____ Administrator   ____ Other(specify) _____

SECTION II

Read the following statements and then indicate whether you agree
or disagree by checking the appropriate box.

	AGREE	DISAGREE

1. In a modern president, an urban background is preferable   1.☐   ☐
to a small-town or rural background.

2. A president who is obdurate is preferable to one who is too   2.☐   ☐
easily swayed.

3. The president should in all instances enforce Supreme   3.☐   ☐
Court decisions.

4. Marital infidelity, while in office is unacceptable   4.☐   ☐
behavior in a president.

5. Sincerity in a president is preferable to charisma.   5.☐   ☐

6. A person possessing religious faith is preferable to   6.☐   ☐
an atheist or agnostic in the White House.

7. The presidential image (i.e., how he looks) is fully as important 7.☐   ☐
to the overall success of a president as are his capabilities.

8. A president should monitor closely the activities of   8.☐   ☐
his friends and relatives while he is in office.

9. Education is not a reliable indicator of presidential performance. 9.☐   ☐

10. Age has little or no significance in relation to   10.☐   ☐
presidential performance.

11. The degree of involvement of the vice-president in the   11.☐   ☐
administration should be solely the president's decision.

12. Honesty in a president is not always the best policy   12.☐   ☐
for the nation.

13. A president should not always be downgraded for failing to   13.☐   ☐
fulfill specific campaign promises once in office.

14. The president has a right to demand that the courts "follow   14.☐   ☐
the election returns" (i.e., that they do not negate the president's
electoral mandate to undertake specific actions).

15. A president who has been a member of congress is apt to be   15.☐   ☐
more successful with congress than one who has not been a member.

16. It would be healthier for the country if every president had some 16.☐   ☐
influential newspaper to act as, and be known as, the administration's
"spokesman".

17. Keeping his party together is more important for a president's   17.☐   ☐
overall success, in the long run, than passing his programs.

18. A president should be judged, at least partially,   18.☐   ☐
on the basis of the friends he has.

19. Even during the times when the opposition party   19.☐   ☐
controls congress, a president should be permitted to
have passed and see enacted his domestic program.
****

Read the following statements and check the appropriate box to
indicate your agreement or disagreement with the question.

	YES	NO

20. Do you agree that an academician would   20.☐   ☐
generally make a poor presidential risk?

21. Do you agree that a president who shoots from the   21.☐   ☐
hip is better than one who continually holds his fire?

PAGE 4   YES   NO

22. It has been said that a president's historical rating   22.☐   ☐
depends ultimately on his ability to represent and form
the conscience of the nation. Do you agree?

23. Do you agree that a deeply committed religious believer is apt to   23.☐   ☐
make a better president than one who is not so deeply committed?

24. Do you agree that, as a rule, wartime presidents   24.☐   ☐
are more highly regarded than peacetime presidents?

25. Do you agree that a president should refuse to enforce a law   25.☐   ☐
if, in his judgement, it is in the national interest to do so?

26. Do you agree that a president has the right to demand press   26.☐   ☐
self-censorship in the interests of national security?

27. Do you agree that, although constitutional,   27.☐   ☐
a 35 year-old is too young to be president?

28. Do you agree that of all branches of government,   28.☐   ☐
the presidency should be the most powerful?

29. Do you agree that a president has a moral obligation   29.☐   ☐
to try to fulfill his campaign promises?

30. Do you agree that, all things considered, a presidential   30.☐   ☐
candidate who is married is preferable to one who is not?

31. Do you agree that a president has the right to   31.☐   ☐
choose his running mate regardless of the wishes of party
leaders or of the nominating convention?

32. Do you agree that in important matters of dispute between the   32.☐   ☐
president and congress, the congress should defer to the president?

33. Do you agree that modern presidents should possess at least a   33.☐   ☐
four-year college degree?

34. Do you agree that a president has the right to   34.☐   ☐
nominate and place qualified judges in the federal
judiciary who reflect his economic and social philosophies?

35. Do you agree that in view of modern presidents' difficulties   35.☐   ☐
with the bureaucracy, the nation should have fewer persons in civil
service and more in presidentially appointed posts?

36. Do you agree that a person over 70 is too old to be president?   36.☐   ☐

37. Do you agree that in the end, presidential success depends as   37.☐   ☐
much on tenacity and determination as on specific programs?
****

Please answer the following by placing a check on the line which
indicates your relative degree of acceptance or non-acceptance
of the statement.

	Agree Totally				Disagree Totally

38. Economically self-made individuals are
generally too self-centered and insensitive   1   2   3   4   5   6
to be good presidents.

39. Partisan politics in congress should
play only a limited role in modifying or
negating a president's foreign policy.   1   2   3   4   5   6

40. Despite claims to the contrary, the
TV media has not skewed presidential
performance from substance to style.   1   2   3   4   5   6

41. An individual trained in the social sciences
will generally make a better president than one
trained in the physical or natural sciences.

| 1 | 2 | 3 | 4 | 5 | 6 |

42. As the people's representative, the president
should be sensitive to public opinion polls and
modify his policies and behavior accordingly.

| 1 | 2 | 3 | 4 | 5 | 6 |

43. To be an effective president requires a large
amount of cunning.

| 1 | 2 | 3 | 4 | 5 | 6 |

****

Please answer the following by placing a check on the line which indicates
your relative degree of acceptance or non-acceptance of the statement,
with a 4 representing neutrality.

                                          Agree   Disagree
                                          Totally   Totally

44. Persons educated in private schools
are generally better prepared for the presidency
than those educated in public schools.

| 1 | 2 | 3 | 4 | 5 | 6 | 7 |

45. Concentration of the media in the hands of
a few organizations has had a deleterious effect
on presidential decision-making.

| 1 | 2 | 3 | 4 | 5 | 6 | 7 |

46. Absence of a heterosexual preference
in a presidential candidate, if known, should be
a critical campaign issue.

| 1 | 2 | 3 | 4 | 5 | 6 | 7 |

47. A person should not allow his religious
beliefs to influence his actual performance as
president.

| 1 | 2 | 3 | 4 | 5 | 6 | 7 |

48. A rich person from a wealthy background
makes a better president than a person from
more modest financial circumstances.

| 1 | 2 | 3 | 4 | 5 | 6 | 7 |

49. It is doubtful if a mostly male congress
would work as well with a female president,
even if she could be elected, as it would with
a male president of equal ability.

| 1 | 2 | 3 | 4 | 5 | 6 | 7 |

****

Please answer the following questions according to the instructions
provided for each one.

50. The nation as a whole would be more receptive to (choose one):
    ____ a black male as president.
    ____ a white female as president.
51. Overall success or failure as a president depends more on (choose one):
    ____ his ability to act as spokesman for the conscience of the nation.
    ____ his ability to help form the conscience of the nation.

52. Check the highest number of divorces you would find acceptable in a presidential candidate (check one):

    —0—   —1—   —2—   —3 or more.

53. All things being equal, would you rather have a president who was skillful in: (check one)
_____ domestic policy?
_____ foreign policy?

54. It is better for a president to have (check one):
_____ a vice-president who is loyal.
_____ a vice-president who exercises independent judgment.

55. The president should treat the expansion of civil rights as (check only one):
_____ an ethical and moral matter involving education to change the minds of citizens.
_____ a judicial and legal matter involving federal enforcement to eliminate abuses.
_____ a state and local matter which should remain outside the interest of the federal government.

56. It may be justified and proper for a president to give misleading information to (check as many as you agree with):
_____ protect his domestic policy
_____ protect his reputation
_____ protect his foreign policy
_____ protect the effectiveness of a skilled and needed advisor
_____ protect national security
_____ a president should not give misleading information.

57. In general, in dealing with his advisors and subordinates, a president should insist on (RANK these in order of preference, with 1 indicating the most preferable quality, 2 the next most preferable and so on):
_____ truthfulness   _____ intelligence
_____ loyalty   _____ political experience
_____ independent judgment

58. The best prior experience for a president is to have been a (RANK the following 1 thru 6, with 1 indicating the best, 2 indicating the next best and so on):
_____ military officer   _____ state governor
_____ cabinet official   _____ vice-president
_____ senator   _____ congressman

59. The presidential image is a product of (RANK the following 1 thru 5, with 1 being the most contributory to his image, 2 the next most contributory and so on):
_____ the president's character   _____ the media
_____ administration policies   _____ presidential style
_____ White House public relations

60. It may be justified and proper for a president to use leaks (check as many as you agree with):
_____ to further a diplomatic effort
_____ to readjust the stock market to aid the nation's economy
_____ to put his political enemies on the defensive
_____ to aid the passage of a favored bill
_____ a president should never use leaks.

61. Listed below are some of the major presidential functions. RANK
them, 1 thru 8, according to your view of their importance, with one
being the most important, 2 the next most important, and so on.

_____	foreign policy planner	_____	head of state
_____	symbolic national spokesman	_____	party leader
_____	primary law enforcer	_____	commander-in-chief
_____	domestic policy initiator	_____	executive administrator

62. RANK the following, 1 thru 6, in order of their importance
as desirable traits in a president (use 1 for the most
desirable, 2 for the next most desirable and so on):

_____	aggressiveness	_____	humaneness
_____	intelligence	_____	honesty
_____	creativity	_____	adaptability

63. In light of the modern world, a modern president should have
knowledge of the following: (use 1 for all those you believe are important,
a 2 for those which are somewhat less important, a 3 for those marginally
important, and a 4 for those which are unnecessary)

_____	Economics	_____	International law
_____	Natural or physical science	_____	Political science
_____	Military Science	_____	other cultures
_____	American history		

64. Listed below are some occupations. RATE them according to
their suitability as training backgrounds for the presidency
(use a 1 to denote very suitable, a 2 for suitable, a 3 for
marginally suitable, and a 4 for unsuitable):

_____	union leader	_____	corporate executive
_____	banker	_____	doctor
_____	engineer	_____	lawyer
_____	journalist	_____	church leader

65. Could there be an ultimate situation in which the president should
be able to order the assassination of (check those with which you agree):

_____ a foreign arch-enemy of the U.S. while at peace
_____ a foreign arch-enemy of the U.S. while at war
_____ a heinous violator of human rights (one practicing
genocide, for example)
_____ a domestic leader of a terrorist group
_____ a foreign leader of a terrorist group
_____ a president should never order assassination

66. A president should use appropriate force (including troops if
necessary) to suppress internal dissent which (check those with which you agree)

_____ is directed toward the violent overthrow of the government
_____ uses physical force to halt the workings of government
_____ involves the destruction of private and public property
_____ threatens the civil or voting rights of citizens
_____ seriously undermines the administration's domestic or foreign policies
_____ a president should never use force to suppress dissent.

PAGE 8

67. A president should be able to interfere in the affairs of another nation
(place a check on the line which most clearly represents your position):

	Never	By means other than military	Militarily
a. to protect a vital American defense interest in a strategic area	_____	_____	_____
b. to protect a vital American economic interest in a strategic area	_____	_____	_____
c. to overthrow a rabid anti-U.S. military dictatorship in a strategic area	_____	_____	_____
d. to overthrow a popularly-established rabid anti-U.S. government in a strategic area	_____	_____	_____

68. A president who (check the line in the column most conforming to
your position):

	Would not bother me	Would bother me some	Would bother me greatly
a. uses public money to refurbish his home as a second White House	_____	_____	_____
b. uses inside presidential information to help family members increase their financial worth	_____	_____	_____
c. appoints family members to high public office, if basically qualified	_____	_____	_____
d. puts relatives or close friends on the public payroll in non-policy making positions	_____	_____	_____

69. An ex-president who (again check the line in the column most conforming
to your position):

	Would not bother me	Would bother me some	Would bother me greatly
a. makes money from his memoirs	_____	_____	_____
b. makes money as a business consultant or director	_____	_____	_____
c. gives paid lectures	_____	_____	_____
d. sells his name to endorse a commercial product	_____	_____	_____
e. receives stipends from talk shows or TV interviews	_____	_____	_____
f. runs again for public office in some other position	_____	_____	_____

****

HISTORIANS whose specialties lie in the period PRIOR TO 1865
proceed to page 9

HISTORIANS whose specialties lie in the period AFTER 1865 proceed
to page 12

NON-HISTORIANS proceed to page 15

SECTION III
Part A
(To be answered only by those historians whose specialties lie in the period
before 1865.)

Please answer the following statements by checking either "yes" or "no"

	YES	NO
1. Do you believe that Jefferson's involvement with slavery on a personal basis (i.e., his ownership of slaves, etc.) should affect his rating as president?	1.☐	☐
2. Do you agree that Lincoln's physical appearance would have excluded him from consideration as a presidential candidate in the modern media age?	2.☐	☐
3. Do you agree with Jackson's ideas concerning rotation in public office (i.e., the spoils system) within the context of the period?	3.☐	☐
4. Do you believe that it was proper for John Q. Adams to reenter congress as a representative after having been president?	4.☐	☐
5. Do you agree that Van Buren's failure to curb American private assistance to Canadian rebels in 1837 was actually in the American interest?	5.☐	☐
6. Do you agree with Buchanan that the president should not have strongly reenforced Ft. Sumter, but should have waited for negotiations instead?	6.☐	☐
7. Do you agree with Jackson's removal of federal deposits from the Second U.S. Bank and their transfer to state banks?	7.☐	☐
8. Do you agree with John Q. Adams's national approach to American problems (e.g., his support for national aid to transportation, a national university and so on)?	8.☐	☐
9. Do you agree with Polk's unilateral action in sending General Taylor and his army to claim the Rio Grande as the boundary of Texas?	9.☐	☐
10. Do you agree that Fillmore should not have acquiesced in the Compromise of 1850 in view of the fact that it incorporated a more stringent fugitive slave law?	10.☐	☐

****

Please indicate by checking the appropriate box whether you agree or
disagree with each of the following statements.

	AGREE	DISAGREE
11. Van Buren should have used direct government intervention to alleviate the economic distress resulting from the Panic of 1837.	11.☐	☐
12. Madison should not have acquiesed in the War of 1812, but should have continued Jefferson's economic sanctions instead.	12.☐	☐
13. Lincoln's inability to find and name competent generals must be rated as a grave weakness of his presidency.	13.☐	☐
14. Jackson's Maysville Road veto was correct in that it prevented the use of federal funds for purely local purposes.	14.☐	☐

PAGE 10   AGREE   DISAGREE

15. Washington should not have used military power in   15.☐   ☐
handling the Whiskey Rebellion in western Pennsylvania.
16. Adams's methods of suppressing internal dissent   16.☐   ☐
(Alien and Sedition Acts) in time of undeclared
war were proper under the circumstances.
17. Jefferson's methods of attacking the federal judiciary   17.☐   ☐
were proper given the nature and magnitude of the
differences between him and the Federalist opposition.
18. Washington's use of cabinet members as personal   18.☐   ☐
policy advisors (in contrast with the use of
the modern cabinet) was a good procedure.
19. Pierce should not have signed the Kansas–Nebraska   19.☐   ☐
Act, opening a territory to slavery which had
been closed previously by the Missouri Compromise.
20. The Monroe administration would have acted in   20.☐   ☐
the national interest if it had censured Jackson
for his Florida military activities.
21. Washington's lack of humor and his aloofness would have   21.☐   ☐
made him an unlikely presidential candidate in the modern period.
22. Madison had the necessary training and experience to be an   22.☐   ☐
outstanding president.
23. Jefferson was not acting in the national interest when he   23.☐   ☐
used force against the Barbary pirates instead of paying tribute.
24. Jackson was correct in threatening to use force in   24.☐   ☐
the South Carolina Nullification Controversy.
25. Lincoln's suspension of the writ of habeas corpus during   25.☐   ☐
the Civil War was justified.
****
Please answer the following by placing a check on the line which indicates
your relative degree of acceptance or non-acceptance of the statement.

                                     Agree   Disagree
                                  Completely   Completely
26. Jackson should not have defied the Supreme
Court on the question of Indian removal.
                                  ‾1‾ ‾2‾ ‾3‾ ‾4‾ ‾5‾ ‾6‾

27. As Harrison's vice-president, Tyler
had a responsibility to follow Harrison's
programs and the party leaders, even though
he disagreed with them.
                                  ‾1‾ ‾2‾ ‾3‾ ‾4‾ ‾5‾ ‾6‾

28. Lincoln's reaction in the early
days of the war to southern secession
was too indecisive and unrealistic.
                                  ‾1‾ ‾2‾ ‾3‾ ‾4‾ ‾5‾ ‾6‾

29. Madison should not have allowed his
wife, Dolley, to exercise so much influence
in his administration.
                                  ‾1‾ ‾2‾ ‾3‾ ‾4‾ ‾5‾ ‾6‾

30. Buchanan's efforts on behalf of the Kansas proslavery
Lecompton Constitution would have been justified
if they would have prevented civil war.
                                  ‾1‾ ‾2‾ ‾3‾ ‾4‾ ‾5‾ ‾6‾

114   Appendixes

31. Taylor's proposal to organize the Mexican
Cession immediately into states in order to
avoid the question of slavery in the
terrritories should have been followed.

$$\overline{1}\quad\overline{2}\quad\overline{3}\quad\overline{4}\quad\overline{5}\quad\overline{6}$$

32. Polk's campaign pledge of "54-40 or Fight"
regarding the Oregon settlement was justifiably
abandoned after the election.

$$\overline{1}\quad\overline{2}\quad\overline{3}\quad\overline{4}\quad\overline{5}\quad\overline{6}$$

33. Washington should not have issued the
Proclamation of Neutrality (1793) in view of
the Franco-American Treaty of Alliance of 1778.

$$\overline{1}\quad\overline{2}\quad\overline{3}\quad\overline{4}\quad\overline{5}\quad\overline{6}$$

34. The modern practice of summitry is
a better procedure than the practice of
early presidents in appointing special
representatives or delegations to
conclude treaties.

$$\overline{1}\quad\overline{2}\quad\overline{3}\quad\overline{4}\quad\overline{5}\quad\overline{6}$$

35. Please RATE below those traits or qualities you believe were most
important for a president's overall success during this period of
American history (use 1 for very important, 2 for important, 3 for
marginally important and 4 for not important at all):

___ intense patriotism	___ integrity
___ an aristocratic bearing	___ previous political experience
___ a pleasing physical appearance	___ intelligence
___ sensitivity to popular demands	___ charisma

****
NOTE
After completing this section, you should proceed to page 15 (SKIP PAGES 12-14).

PAGE 12

SECTION III
Part B
(To be answered only by those historians whose specialties lie in
the period after 1865.)

Please answer the the following questions by checking either "yes" or "no".

	YES	NO
1. Do you agree that Franklin Roosevelt should not have run for a third term in 1940?	1.□	□
2. Do you agree with Theodore Roosevelt that "good ends" sometimes must take precedent over means (as in the case of conservation).	2.□	□
3. Do you agree with Coolidge's contention that lower taxes on high incomes frees capital for industrial expansion and creates jobs?	3.□	□
4. Do you agree with Wilson's view that a president should play an active role in shaping his party's congressional program?	4.□	□
5. Do you agree with McKinley that the president's duty on the issue of war and peace is simply to present the case (as with the Cuban situation in 1898) and allow congress to determine the outcome?	5.□	□
6. Do you agree that congress should be able to remove a president because of grave political and philosophical differences if, as in the case of Andrew Johnson, he loses his ability to govern?	6.□	□
7. Do you agree with Harding and Coolidge that presidents should leave cabinet officials alone to handle their own departments?	7.□	□
8. Do you agree with Wilson's use of non-recognition as a foreign policy weapon to influence the change of leadership in a foreign government?	8.□	□
9. Do you agree with Harding that high protective tariffs, especially in such competitive areas as steel, are essential to maintain jobs and the American worker's standard of living?	9.□	□
10. Do you agree with Cleveland that upholding a principle (in his case, low tariffs and sound money) is more important than maintaining party harmony?	10.□	□
11. Do you agree that McKinley acted wisely in recommending the acquisition of the Phillipine islands?	11.□	□
12. Do you agree that if Harding had lived, he should have been impeached because of the corruption in his administration?	12.□	□

****

Please indicate by checking the appropriate box whether or not you agree or disagree with each of the following statements.

	AGREE	DISAGREE
13. Theodore Roosevelt was correct in stating that, if necessary, the U.S. should act unilaterally in Latin America to protect American interests there.	13.□	□
14. Wilson was right to stick by his guns in the League fight of 1919.	14.□	□
15. Hayes's suggestion of a one 6-year term for presidents would be an improvement over the present system.	15.□	□
16. Coolidge had the necessary training and political experience to be an outstanding president.	16.□	□
17. Grant's refusal to support the Fenians in their comflict with the Canadian government was not in the American national interest.	17.□	□

PAGE 13

	AGREE	DISAGREE

18. Theodore Roosevelt was justified in demanding that his hand-picked successor, Taft, continue Roosevelt's Square Deal policies.   18.☐   ☐

19. Franklin Roosevelt acted within the proper prerogatives of the president in his attempt to "pack" the Supreme Court in order to force a change in its decisions.   19.☐   ☐

20. Cleveland's use of troops in the Pullman Strike, in order to prevent the disruption of the mails, was the proper action to take under the circumstances.   20.☐   ☐

21. Although Grant was not personally involved, the scandals of his administrations must be laid at his door.   21.☐   ☐

22. Hayes's decision to pull the troops out of the South in 1877 was the correct action to take, even though it allowed the restoration of white Bourbon supremacy.   22.☐   ☐

23. Taft was correct in stating that party loyalty should take precedent over personal political obligations or policy differences.   23.☐   ☐

24. Hoover was correct in his belief that, in the long run, federal fiscal soundness and a balanced budget are prerequisites to national economic health.   24.☐   ☐

25. Contrary to his action, Cleveland should have arranged for Hawaiian annexation immediately following the Hawaiian Revolution.   25.☐   ☐

26. Grant's indication of his willingness to abide by international arbitration "before the fact," as in the Alabama Claims dispute, was not in the best national interest.   26.☐   ☐

27. Congress should have prevented Theodore Roosevelt's exercise of unilateral executive authority in the Panamanian situation.   27.☐   ☐

28. Hoover was correct in refusing to meet the demands of the Bonus Marchers in 1932.   28.☐   ☐

****

Please answer the following by placing a check on the line which indicates your relative degree of acceptance or non-acceptance of the statement.

         Agree   Disagree
         Completely   Completely

29. Franklin Roosevelt's experience at Yalta and Wilson's at Versailles indicate that the disadvantages of summitry outweigh the probable advantages.

     1   2   3   4   5   6

30. Andrew Johnson was well-prepared for the presidency because of his previous office-holding and broad political experience.

     1   2   3   4   5   6

31. Cleveland should not have used private bankers and private loans to preserve the financial integrity of the U.S. government in 1895.

     1   2   3   4   5   6

32. Even though he did not have the congressional funding to do so, Theodore Roosevelt acted within proper presidential prerogatives in sending the Great White Fleet around the world.

     1   2   3   4   5   6

33. Grant should have openly supported Cuban
independence following the Virginius affair.

$\overline{}\,\overline{}\,\overline{}\,\overline{}\,\overline{}\,\overline{}$
  1   2   3   4   5   6

34. Franklin Roosevelt was wrong in using the
vice-presidency as a political pawn and
largely ignoring the man holding that position
during his years in office.

  1   2   3   4   5   6

35. Cleveland's handling of Coxey's
army was too insensitive and harsh.

  1   2   3   4   5   6

36. Please RATE below those traits
or qualities which you believe were most important for a president's
overall success during this period (use 1 for very important, 2 for
important, 3 for marginally important, and 4 for not important at all.):

    ___ intense patriotism   ___ integrity
    ___ an aristocratic bearing   ___ previous political experience
    ___ a pleasing physical appearance ___ intelligence
    ___ sensitivity to popular demands ___ charisma

NOTE: Please continue to page 15 (Section III, Part C)

Section III
Part C
(since 1945 -- to be answered by all respondents)

Please answer the following questions by checking either "yes" or "no"

	YES	NO
1. Do you agree with Truman's intervention in Korea in 1950?	1.□	□
2. Do you agree with Carter's decentralized approach to the White House administrative structure?	2.□	□
3. Do you agree with Truman's early support of and recognition of Israel?	3.□	□
4. Do you agree that Ford acted in the national interest by pardoning Nixon before a trial?	4.□	□
5. Do you agree that in order to preserve Russian-American summit negotiations, Eisenhower should not have taken personal blame for the U-2 affair?	5.□	□
6. Do you agree that in view of his campaign promises in 1968, Nixon's retention of American forces in Vietnam deserves condemnation?	6.□	□
7. Do you agree that on the basis of education and administrative experience, Truman was not prepared for the presidency?	7.□	□
8. Do you agree that as president, Ford displayed too limited an intellect for the job?	8.□	□
9. Do you agree with Truman's removal of MacArthur in 1951?	9.□	□
10. Do you agree that Johnson acted properly in advocating the expenditure of federal funds for local pollution control?	10.□	□
11. Do you agree that Nixon should have resigned his office because of Watergate?	11.□	□

****

Please indicate by checking the appropriate box whether you agree or disagree with each of the following statements.

	AGREE	DISAGREE
12. Carter was correct in not intervening militarily (except for the rescue mission) in the Iranian hostage situation.	12.□	□
13. On the basis of administrative and political experience, Kennedy was well-prepared for the presidency.	13.□	□
14. Truman was wrong in being so inflexible in his domestic and civil rights policies as to permit a party split in 1948.	14.□	□
15. Nixon's attempt to bring the White House hierarchy under more direct and organized supervision was a realistic response to modern demands on the presidency.	15.□	□
16. Kennedy should have knocked down the Wall by force in order to prevent the physical partition of Berlin.	16.□	□
17. Nixon's pragmatic and non-ideological approach to foreign policy was too Machiavellian for the American democratic system to sustain for long.	17.□	□
18. By political background and experience, Johnson was well-prepared for the presidency.	18.□	□
19. Ford's image as president was too often the product of distorted media coverage.	19.□	□
20. Nixon's imposition of wage-price controls to combat inflation was the correct course of action to take and he should have stuck with them.	20.□	□

PAGE 16

AGREE   DISAGREE

21. Although he was not personally involved , the corruption   21.☐   ☐
in Truman's administration must be laid at his door.
22. Nixon had a right to nominate and place on the Supreme   22.☐   ☐
Court justices who conformed to his socio-economic views,
including those on race relations and law and order.
23. Eisenhower should not have allowed the U.S. to cast a   23.☐   ☐
UN vote to condemn England, France and Israel in the Suez
Crisis of 1956.
****

Please answer the following by placing a check on the line which
indicates your relative degree of acceptance or non-acceptance
of the statement.

Agree   Disagree
Completely   Completely

24. Carter should somehow have arranged
for the delivery of arms and other
military support for the Afghan rebels.   ‾1‾ ‾2‾ ‾3‾ ‾4‾ ‾5‾ ‾6‾
25. Nixon should be given high marks for
deescalating the war in Vietnam and
preparing for eventual American withdrawal.
‾1‾ ‾2‾ ‾3‾ ‾4‾ ‾5‾ ‾6‾
26. Although some critics claim he acted tardily,
Eisenhower did finally act properly in using troops
in the Little Rock crisis.
‾1‾ ‾2‾ ‾3‾ ‾4‾ ‾5‾ ‾6‾
27. Kennedy should have given enough
military support to the Cuban insurgents
at the Bay of Pigs to ensure their success.
‾1‾ ‾2‾ ‾3‾ ‾4‾ ‾5‾ ‾6‾
28. Carter's emphasis on human rights
as an integral part of American foreign policy
was in the nation's long-term interest.
‾1‾ ‾2‾ ‾3‾ ‾4‾ ‾5‾ ‾6‾
29. Nixon should have served a jail sentence
if found guilty of the Watergate charges.

‾1‾ ‾2‾ ‾3‾ ‾4‾ ‾5‾ ‾6‾
30. Ford's handling of the Mayaguez incident
was what the situation called for.
‾1‾ ‾2‾ ‾3‾ ‾4‾ ‾5‾ ‾6‾
31. Eisenhower's belief that the U.S. should always
support the UN charter without fail was in the long-
term interest of the nation.
‾1‾ ‾2‾ ‾3‾ ‾4‾ ‾5‾ ‾6‾
32. Kennedy was correct when he claimed, in answering
the Schlesinger poll of 1962, that unless you were
in the president's shoes and knew all the possible
alternatives at the moment of decision, you
cannot judge his actions accurately.
‾1‾ ‾2‾ ‾3‾ ‾4‾ ‾5‾ ‾6‾
****

Please answer the following questions according to the special instructions
    for each one.

33. RATE Johnson as president on (use 1 for a superlative rating, 2 for a good
rating, 3 for a fair rating, 4 for a poor rating, and 5 for a failure):
    ___ his civil rights program   ___ his handling of internal dissent
    ___ his forceful personal tactics ___ his determination
    ___ his homey TV image   ___ his domestic socio-economic plans
34. The following are among those factors often mentioned as contributing to
Nixon's downfall. RATE the following, using 1 as very significant, 2 as
significant, 3 for marginally significant, and 4 for not significant at all:
    ___ the animus of the media   ___ his physical image
    ___ his apparent duplicity   ___ his economic policies
    ___ his use of presidential power ___ the "eastern establishment"
    ___ his Vietnam actions
35. Among the alleged assets of Kennedy were (RATE the following,
 using a 1 for very significant, 2 for significant, 3 for
marginally significant, and 4 for not significant at all:
    ___ his Eastern connections   ___ his ability to inspire
    ___ his youth and vigor   ___ his media relations
    ___ his family wealth   ___ his ability to learn quickly
36. Indicate whether you believe the following are assets or liabilities for
the Truman administration (use a 1 to denote a major asset, 2 for an asset,
3 for unimportant, 4 for a liability, and 5 for a major liability):
    ___ his dropping the atomic bomb ___ his succeeding FDR as president
    ___ his appointees   ___ his "underdog" role
    ___ his attacks on his   ___ his determination
        political opposition   ___ his domestic policies
    ___ his foreign policy
37. What kind of rating would you give Carter on (use a 1 for
superlative rating, 2 for a good rating, 3 for a fair rating,
4 for a poor rating and 5 for a failure):
    ___ his decisiveness   ___ his use of presidential power
    ___ his ability to see the   ___ his relationships with Congress
        large picture   ___ his speaking style
    ___ his personality   ___ his background and training
38. Indicate whether you believe the following are assets or liabilties of
the Eisenhower presidency (use a 1 to denote a major asset, a 2 for an asset,
a 3 for unimportant, a 4 for a liability and a 5 for a major liability):
    ___ his military background   ___ his appointees
    ___ his middle-of-the-road stance ___ his age
    ___ his character   ___ his handling of Eastern
                                            European unrest
39. TV was allegedly a major factor in each of the following: (check
those with which you agree):
    ___ Johnson's refusal to run in 1968
    ___ Ford's loss to Carter in 1976
    ___ Nixon's loss to Kennedy in 1960
    ___ Carter's loss to Reagan in 1980

PAGE 18

40. RANK the following modern presidents to the extent that they practiced
an "imperial" presidency (use 1 for the most "imperial", 2 for the next
most and so on, reserving a "10" for those you consider not "imperial" at all):

    ___ James Carter   ___ John Kennedy
    ___ Dwight Eisenhower   ___ Richard Nixon
    ___ Gerald Ford   ___ Franklin Roosevelt
    ___ Herbert Hoover   ___ Harry Truman
    ___ Lyndon Johnson

41. RANK the following modern presidents with regard to their ability
as an executive administrator (use 1 for the best performance,
2 for the next best, and so on):

    ___ James Carter   ___ John Kennedy
    ___ Dwight Eisenhower   ___ Richard Nixon
    ___ Gerald Ford   ___ Franklin Roosevelt
    ___ Herbert Hoover   ___ Harry Truman
    ___ Lyndon Johnson

42. Please RATE below those traits or qualities you believe were
most important for a president's overall success during this period
of American history (use 1 for very important, 2 for important, 3
for marginally important, and 4 for not important at all):

    ___ intense patriotism   ___ integrity
    ___ an aristocratic bearing ___ previous political experience
    ___ intelligence   ___ a pleasing physical appearance
    ___ charisma   ___ sensitivity to popular demands

****

SECTION IV
(To be completed by all respondents.)

Would you please now take a minute and write down, in preferential order,
your selections for the ten best presidents in the nation's history.
In column two would you please write down in preferential order the
eight modern presidents since Hoover and excluding Reagan.

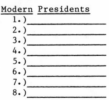

Ten Best Presidents   Modern Presidents

     1.)_____   1.)_____
     2.)_____   2.)_____
     3.)_____   3.)_____
     4.)_____   4.)_____
     5.)_____   5.)_____
     6.)_____   6.)_____
     7.)_____   7.)_____
     8.)_____   8.)_____
     9.)_____
    10.)_____

SECTION IV (Cont.)
(to be completed by all historians -- optional for non-historians)

As a final task, please RATE all the following presidents according to the
Schlesinger categories listed below (William H. Harrison, James Garfield and
Ronald Reagan are excluded because of their brief time in office).

	Great	Near Great	Above Average	Average	Below Average	Failure
John Adams	____	____	____	____	____	____
John Q. Adams	____	____	____	____	____	____
Chester A. Arthur	____	____	____	____	____	____
James Buchanan	____	____	____	____	____	____
James E. Carter	____	____	____	____	____	____
Grover Cleveland	____	____	____	____	____	____
Calvin Coolidge	____	____	____	____	____	____
Dwight Eisenhower	____	____	____	____	____	____
Millard Fillmore	____	____	____	____	____	____
Gerald Ford	____	____	____	____	____	____
Ulysses S. Grant	____	____	____	____	____	____
Benjamin Harrison	____	____	____	____	____	____
Rutherford B. Hayes	____	____	____	____	____	____
Herbert C. Hoover	____	____	____	____	____	____
Warren G. Harding	____	____	____	____	____	____
Andrew Jackson	____	____	____	____	____	____
Lyndon B. Johnson	____	____	____	____	____	____
Andrew Johnson	____	____	____	____	____	____
Thomas Jefferson	____	____	____	____	____	____
John F. Kennedy	____	____	____	____	____	____
Abraham Lincoln	____	____	____	____	____	____
William McKinley	____	____	____	____	____	____
James Madison	____	____	____	____	____	____
James Monroe	____	____	____	____	____	____
Richard Nixon	____	____	____	____	____	____
Franklin Pierce	____	____	____	____	____	____
James K. Polk	____	____	____	____	____	____
Theodore Roosevelt	____	____	____	____	____	____
Franklin Roosevelt	____	____	____	____	____	____
William H. Taft	____	____	____	____	____	____
Zachory Taylor	____	____	____	____	____	____
Harry S Truman	____	____	____	____	____	____
John Tyler	____	____	____	____	____	____
Martin Van Buren	____	____	____	____	____	____
George Washington	____	____	____	____	____	____
Woodrow Wilson	____	____	____	____	____	____

Appendix 2

Presidents Ranked by Controversiality
(As Measured by Standard Deviation)

Rank	President	Standard Deviation of Ratings	Rank	President	Standard Deviation of Ratings
1	Nixon	1.128	19	Tyler	.783
2	L. Johnson	1.066	20	Fillmore	.778
3	Hoover	1.065	21	T. Roosevelt	.777
4	Jackson	1.027	22	Coolidge	.771
5	J. Q. Adams	1.011	23	McKinley	.762
6	A. Johnson	1.004	24	Ford	.761
7	Truman	.993	25	Taft	.758
8	Wilson	.983	26	Monroe	.752
9	Carter	.975	27	Arthur	.746
10	Polk	.975	28	Harding	.737
11	Kennedy	.920	29	Taylor	.732
12	Madison	.913	30	Pierce	.715
13	J. Adams	.880	31	Van Buren	.711
14	Eisenhower	.871	32	Hayes	.683
15	Cleveland	.856	33	B. Harrison	.678
16	Jefferson	.853	34	Washington	.629
17	Grant	.848	35	F. Roosevelt	.586
18	Buchanan	.805	36	Lincoln	.480

Note: One unit of measure is equal to one full category. Hence Richard M. Nixon, Lyndon Johnson, Herbert Hoover, Andrew Jackson, John Quincy Adams, and Andrew Johnson have standard deviations greater than a full category.

Appendix 3

Difference from Mean Rating by Age Groups
of Historians for Presidents
Showing Significant Variations
(α = .05)

	Age Of Historian						
President	65 and over (N = 48)	60-64 (N = 70)	55-59 (N = 95)	50-54 (N = 119)	45-49 (N = 168)	40-44 (N = 181)	39 and Under (N = 130)
Buchanan	.25	.21	.03	.01	-.02	-.06	-.13
Cleveland	.53	.22	.15	.04	-.14	-.11	-.14
Hoover	.30	.08	.29	.02	-.14	-.03	-.17
A. Johnson	.55	.45	.20	.08	-.26	-.14	-.15
Truman	.21	.25	.21	.01	.08	-.10	-.34
Wilson	.22	.41	.10	-.05	.02	-.06	-.26

Note: This table reports the result of subtracting the mean rating given to a
president by each particular age group from the mean rating given that president by
all respondents. It indicates how much a particular age group varies from the
average, and a comparison of the results indicates how much the various groups differ
from each other. For instance, those historians of age 60 and over rate James
Buchanan higher than those of age 50 to 59, and all of these rate him higher than
historians below age 50.

Appendix 4

Mean Rating by Sex of Historian for Presidents
Showing Significant Variations
(α = . 05)

President	Male Rating (N = 787)[a]	Female Rating (N = 59)	Significance Level
Carter	4.39	4.09	.005
Grant	5.28	5.05	.041
L. Johnson	2.90	2.56	.020
Kennedy	3.16	2.85	.014
Polk	3.05	3.46	.002
Washington	1.25	1.59	.007

Note: The higher the score, the lower the evaluation by a specific group.
For instance, the male rating of Jimmy Carter (4.39) is a lower score than
the female rating of Carter (4.09).

[a]Includes the four historians who did not indicate sex.

Appendix 5

Presidents with Significant Differences
in Ratings by Historians'
Regions of Birth and Ph.D.-Granting Institutions
($\propto$ = .05)

	South (N = 97)	Midwest (N = 174)	West (N = 51)
North (N = 136)	Hayes* Fillmore Buchanan A. Johnson Polk* Grant*	Hayes* A. Johnson* Truman Polk*	
West (N = 174)	Buchanan Grant* A. Johnson	A. Johnson	
Midwest (N = 51)	Eisenhower* Buchanan Grant* Polk*		A. Johnson

Note: Where an analysis of variance indicated that historians of one area
differed on a president from historians of at least one other area (at the
.05 level of significance), the Duncan Range, Fisher, and Scheffe
procedures were all used to locate which specific areas differed. If the
Duncan Range and Fisher tests (both adjusted for differing sample sizes)
show that two areas have significant differences (oc = .05), then the
president's name is listed. To find the areas that disagree and which
presidents they disagree on, choose a row or column and notice the
presidents listed at the intersecting columns or rows. For instance,
following the West row across indicates that the West disagrees with the
South on James Buchanan, Ulysses S. Grant, and Andrew Johnson, and that it
disagrees with the Midwest on Andrew Johnson. Following the West column
down shows that the North and the West do not disagree on any president.

*Results obtained from Duncan Range, Fisher, and Scheffe procedures all
show significant differences.

Appendix 6

Difference from Mean Rating by
Subject Specialty of Historian for Presidents
Showing significant Variations
(α = .05)

President	Southern Historians	Afro-American Historians	Military Historians	Women's Historians	Other
Carter	.29*	.44*	-.19	.29	-
A. Johnson	.11	-.65*	-.08	-.01	-
Washington	-.14	-.06	.07	-.58*	-
Jefferson	.05	-.37*	-.06	.09	.37*[a]
Fillmore	.26*	-.16	.10	-.28	-
Eisenhower	-.28*	-.19	.24*	-.27	-
Madison	.04	.10	-.23*	.30	-
Grant	-.28*	.28	-.10	.42*	-
Polk	.36*	-.55*	.09	-.42*	-
T. Roosevelt	.09	-.11	.14	-.35*	-.38*[b]

*Indicates that the group's mean rating significantly deviates from the mean rating by all other historians. For instance, historians who specialize in southern history rank Jimmy Carter significantly higher than historians who do not specialize in southern history. The difference between southern historians' judgement of Carter and all other historians' judgement of Carter is 29 percent of one category.

Appendix 7

Goodness-of-Fit Measures of
Demographic and Scholastic Factors in
Historians' Ratings of Different Presidents

President	Multiple R	R^2	Adjusted R^2	Significance
J. Adams	.166	.027	.024	.0000
J. Q. Adams	.219	.048	.041	.0000
Arthur	.081	.006	.005	.0200
Buchanan	.239	.057	.052	.0000
Carter	.203	.041	.035	.0000
Cleveland	.386	.149	.141	.0000
Coolidge	.160	.025	.023	.0001
Eisenhower	.162	.026	.022	.0002
Fillmore	.126	.015	.013	.0032
Ford	.165	.027	.023	.0002
Grant	.132	.017	.016	.0003
B. Harrison	.119	.014	.011	.0058
Hayes	.182	.033	.027	.0001
Hoover	.129	.016	.013	.0024
Harding	.080	.006	.005	.0309
Jackson	.127	.016	.013	.0029
L. Johnson	.087	.117	.006	.0188
A. Johnson	.305	.093	.087	.0000
Jefferson	.139	.019	.016	.0009
Kennedy	.120	.014	.011	.0054
Lincoln	.128	.016	.013	.0026
McKinley	.198	.039	.035	.0000
Madison	.191	.036	.029	.0001
Monroe	.204	.041	.034	.0000
Nixon	.073	.005	.004	.0482
Pierce	.192	.037	.031	.0000
Polk	.247	.061	.054	.0000
T. Roosevelt	.108	.011	.010	.0036
F. Roosevelt	.138	.019	.017	.0002
Taft	.209	.043	.037	.0000
Truman	.239	.057	.050	.0000
Tyler	.122	.015	.012	.0043
Van Buren	.145	.021	.018	.0005
Washington	.134	.018	.016	.0003
Wilson	.200	.040	.035	.0000

Note: Independent variables relating to sex, regional characteristics, and
subject speciality of historians were treated as zero-one dummy variables.
Independent variables relating to age, number of publications, and area of
concentration (time period) were treated as interval variables. The plot of
the predicted values versus the residual values showed no clear model
inadequacies for any one president, and a suppression of outliers with
standardized residual alues greater than 4.0 did not greatly improve a model's
fit for any one president.

Appendix 8

A Ranking in Order of Importance of Eight Factors Contributing
to Presidential Success in Various
Time Periods

	Time Periods		
	1789-1865	1865-1945	Since 1945
Integrity	1	2	2
Intelligence	2	1	1
Previous Political Experience	3	3	5
Sensitivity to Popular Demands	4	4	3
Intense Patriotism	5	6	7
Charisma	6	5	4
An Aristocratic Bearing	7	8	8
A Pleasing Physical Appearance	8	7	6

*See also Appendix 1, Section III, Part A, 35; Part B, 36; and Part c, 42

Appendix 9A

President	Date of Birth	Birth Place	Age When Inaugurated	Age at Death	Number of Marriages	Religion	Education	Primary Occupation or Profession
Washington 1789–1797	February 22, 1732	Pope's Creek VA	57	67	1	Episcopalian	Non-Formal	Planation Owner
J. Adams 1797–1801	October 30, 1735	Quincy, MA	61	90	1	Congregationalist	Harvard	Lawyer
Jefferson 1801–1809	April 13, 1743	Albemarle Co., VA	57	83	1	Non-formal	William & Mary	Lawyer
Madison 1809–1817	March 16, 1751	King's Co. VA	57	85	1	Episcopalian	College of New Jersey	Lawyer
Monroe 1817–1825	April 28, 1758	Westmoreland Co., VA	58	73	1	Episcopalian	William & Mary	Lawyer
J. Q. Adams 1825–1829	July 11, 1767	Quincy, MA	57	80	1	Unitarian	Harvard	Lawyer
Jackson 1829–1837	March 15, 1767	Waxhaw, SC/NC	61	78	1	Presbyterian	Non-Formal	Military Leader
Van Buren 1837–1841	December 5, 1782	Kinderhook, NY	54	79	1	Dutch-Reformed	Nonformal	Lawyer
W. H. Harrison 1841	February 9, 1773	Charles City Co., VA	68	68	1	Episcopalian	Hampton-Sydney College	Military Leader
Tyler 1841–1845	March 29, 1790	Near Williamsburg, VA	51	71	2	Episcopalian	William & Mary	Lawyer
Polk 1845–1849	November 2, 1795	Near Pineville, NC	49	53	1	Presbyterian	University of N.C.	Lawyer
Taylor 1849–1850	November 24, 1784	Montebello, VA	64	65	1	Episcopalian	Non-Formal	Military Leader
Fillmore 1850–1853	January 7, 1800	Cayuga, Co. NY	50	74	2	Unitarian	Non-Formal	Lawyer
Pierce 1853–1857	November 23, 1804	Hillsborough NH	48	64	1	Episcopalian	Bowdoin College	Lawyer
Buchanan 1857–1861	April 23, 1791	Cove Gap, PA	65	77	0	Presbyterian	Dickinson College	Lawyer
Lincoln 1861–1865	February 12, 1809	Hardin, Co., KY	52	56	1	Non-Formal	Non-Formal	Lawyer
A. Johnson 1865–1869	December 29, 1808	Raleigh, NC	56	66	1	Non-Formal	Non-Formal	Politician
Grant 1869–1877	April 27, 1822	Point Pleasant OH	46	63	1	Methodist	West Point	Military Leader
Hayes 1877–1881	October 4, 1822	Delaware, OH	54	70	1	Methodist	Kenyon College	Lawyer

President	Date of Birth	Birth Place	Age When Inaugurated	Age at Death	Number of Marriages	Religion	Education	Primary Occupation or Profession
Garfield 1881	November 19, 1831	Cuyahoga, Co., OH	49	49	1	Disciples of Christ	Williams College	Lawyer
Arthur 1881-1885	October 5, 1830	Fairfield, VT	51	56	1	Episcopalian	Union College, NY	Lawyer
Cleveland 1885-1889 1893-1897	March 18, 1837	Caldwell, NJ	47	71	1	Presbyterian	Non-Formal	Lawyer
B. Harrison 1889-1893	August 20, 1833	North Bend, OH	55	67	1	Presbyterian	Miami University	Lawyer
McKinley 1893-1901	January 29, 1843	Niles, OH	54	58	1	Methodist	Allegheny College	Lawyer
T. Roosevelt 1901-1909	October 27, 1858	NY City, NY	42	60	1	Dutch Reformed	Harvard	Politician
Taft 1909-1913	September 15, 1857	Cincinnati, OH	51	72	1	Unitarian	Yale	Lawyer
Wilson 1913-1921	December 29, 1856	Staunton, VA	56	67	2	Presbyterian	Princeton	Academician
Harding 1921-1923	November 2, 1865	Blooming Grove, OH	55	57	1	Baptist	OH Central College	Journalist
Coolidge 1923-1929	July 4, 1872	Plymouth Notch, VT	51	60	1	Congregational	Amherst	Lawyer
Hoover 1929-1933	August 10, 1874	West Branch, IA	54	90	1	Quaker	Stanford	Engineer
F. Roosevelt 1933-1945	January 30, 1882	Hyde Park, NY	51	63	1	Episcopalian	Harvard	Politician
Truman 1945-1953	May 8, 1884	Lamar, MO	60	88	1	Baptist	High School	Politician
Eisenhower 1953-1961	October 14, 1890	Denison, TX	62	78	1	Presbyterian	West Point	Military Leader
Kennedy 1961-1963	May 24, 1917	Brookline, MA	43	46	1	Catholic	Harvard	Politician
L. Johnson 1963-1969	August 27, 1908	Stonewall, TX	55	64	1	Disciples of Christ	SW TX State Teachers	Rancher
Nixon 1969-1974	January 9, 1913	Yorba Linda, CA	56		1	Quaker	Whittier College	Lawyer
Ford 1974-1977	July 14, 1913	Omaha, NE	61		1	Episcopalian	Univ. of Michigan	Lawyer
Carter 1977-1981	October 1, 1924	Plains, GA	52		1	Baptist	Annapolis	Farmer
Reagan 1981-	February 6, 1911	Tampico, IL	69		2	Episcopalian	Eureka College	Actor

Appendix 9B

President	Ancestory	War Veteran	Diplomat	Member of Congress	State Legislature	Governor	Cabinet Member	Vice-President
Washington 1789–1797	English	X			X			
J. Adams 1797–1801	English		X	X	X			X
Jefferson 1801–1809	Welsh		X	X	X	X	X	X
Madison 1809–1817	English			X	X		X	
Monroe 1917–1825	Scotch	X	X	X	X	X	X	
J. Q. Adams 1825–1829	English		X	X			X	
Jackson 1829–1837	Scotch/Irish	X		X		X		
Van Buren 1837–1841	Dutch		X	X	X	X	X	X
W. H. Harrison 1841	English	X	X	X	X	X1	X	
Tyler 1841–1845	English			X	X	X		X
Polk 1845–1849	Scotch/Irish			X	X	X		
Taylor 1849–1850	English	X						
Fillmore 1850–1853	English			X	X			X
Pierce 1853–1857	English			X	X			
Buchanan 1857–1861	Scotch/Irish		X	X	X		X	
Lincoln 1861–1865	English			X	X			
A. Johnson 1865–1869	English			X	X	X		X
Grant 1869–1877	English	X					X	
Hayes 1877–1881	Scotch	X		X	X	X		

President	Ancestry	War Veteran	Diplomat	Member of Congress	State Legislature	Governor	Cabinet Member	Vice-President
Garfield 1881	English	X		X	X			
Arthur 1881–1885	Scotch/ Irish							X
Cleveland 1885–1889 1893–1897	English					X		
B. Harrison 1889–1893	English	X		X				
McKinley 1893–1901	Scotch/ Irish	X		X		X		
T. Roosevelt 1901–1909	Dutch	X			X	X		X
Taft 1909–1913	English					X2	X	
Wilson 1913–1921	Scotch/ Irish					X		
Harding 1921–1923	English			X	X			
Coolidge 1923–1929	English				X	X		X
Hoover 1929–1933	Swiss/ German						X	
F. Roosevelt 1933–1945	Dutch				X	X		
Truman 1945–1953	Scotch/ Irish	X		X				X
Eisenhower 1953–1961	Swiss/ German	X						
Kennedy 1961–1963	Irish	X		X				
L. Johnson 1963–1969	English			X				X
Nixon 1969–1974	Scotch/ Irish			X				X
Ford 1974–1977	English	X		X				X
Carter 1977–1981	English				X	X		
Reagan 1981–	Irish					X		

Appendix 10

Least Aggressive Versus Most Aggressive Historians

Least Aggressive (N = 173)				Most Aggressive (N = 160)		
Rank	President	Rating		Rank	President	Rating
1	Lincoln	(1.21)		1	Lincoln	(1.12)
2	F. D. Roosevelt	(1.26)		2	Washington	(1.18)
3	Washington	(1.47)		3	F. D. Roosevelt	(1.33)
4	Jefferson	(1.77)		4	Jefferson	(1.70)
5	T. Roosevelt	(2.25)		5	T. Roosevelt	(1.73)
6	Wilson	(2.35)		6	Wilson	(2.07)
7	Jackson	(2.65)		7	Jackson	(2.19)
8	J. Adams	(2.91)		8	Truman	(2.20)
9	L. Johnson	(2.96)		9	Polk	(2.76)
10	Eisenhower	(3.08)		10	J. Adams	(2.83)
11	Truman	(3.09)		11	L. Johnson	(2.99)
12	Kennedy	(3.18)			Eisenhower	(2.99)
13	Madison	(3.24)		13	Madison	(3.28)
14	Monroe	(3.30)			Monroe	(3.28)
	J. Q. Adams	(3.30)		15	Kennedy	(3.30)
16	Polk	(3.55)		16	Cleveland	(3.34)
17	Cleveland	(3.64)		17	J. Q. Adams	(3.56)
18	McKinley	(3.86)		18	McKinley	(3.68)
19	Van Buren	(3.91)		19	Taft	(3.75)
20	Taft	(4.03)		20	Hoover	(3.88)
21	Carter	(4.14)		21	Hayes	(4.00)
22	Hayes	(4.18)		22	Van Buren	(4.06)
	Hoover	(4.18)		23	Ford	(4.12)
24	Arthur	(4.36)		24	Arthur	(4.14)
25	Harrison	(4.44)		25	Harrison	(4.33)
26	Taylor	(4.45)		26	Coolidge	(4.443)
27	Ford	(4.60)		27	Taylor	(4.49)
28	Tyler	(4.73)		28	Fillmore	(4.60)
29	Fillmore	(4.74)			Tyler	(4.60)
30	Coolidge	(4.88)		30	Carter	(4.70)
31	Pierce	(5.02)		31	Nixon	(4.78)
32	Grant	(5.11)		32	Pierce	(4.87)
33	Buchanan	(5.23)		33	A. Johnson	(4.94)
34	A. Johnson	(5.31)		34	Buchanan	(5.09)
35	Harding	(5.54)		35	Grant	(5.30)
36	Nixon	(5.59)		36	Harding	(5.58)

Note: In terms of methodology, some caution should be observed when using this table. The Murray-Blessing survey was not designed specifically to analyze certain very basic personal beliefs held by historians, and we do not believe that anything but the simple analysis supplied here should be implied or inferred from our data. The question of the interplay of personal beliefs and historical analysis demands much more direct examination than is afforded by our survey.

Appendix 11

Most Conservative Versus Most Liberal on Domestic Socio-Economic Issues

	Conservatives (N = 50)			Liberals (N = 190)	
Rank	President	Rating	Rank	President	Rating
1	Lincoln	(1.29)	1	Lincoln	(1.10)
2	Washington	(1.36)	2	F. Roosevelt	(1.17)
3	F. Roosevelt	(1.62)	3	Washington	(1.30)
4	Jefferson	(1.78)	4	Jefferson	(1.60)
5	T. Roosevelt	(1.84)	5	T. Roosevelt	(1.96)
6	Jackson	(2.44)	6	Wilson	(1.98)
7	Truman	(2.48)	7	Jackson	(2.32)
8	Wilson	(2.50)	8	Truman	(2.48)
9	Eisenhower	(2.90)	9	L. Johnson	(2.70)
10	J. Adams	(2.98)	10	J. Adams	(2.84)
11	Polk	(3.04)	11	Kennedy	(3.11)
12	L. Johnson	(3.28)	12	Eisenhower	(3.12)
	Cleveland	(3.28)	13	Polk	(3.22)
14	J. Q. Adams	(3.32)	14	Madison	(3.29)
	Madison	(3.32)	15	Monroe	(3.36)
	Monroe	(3.32)	16	J. Q. Adams	(3.46)
17	Hoover	(3.52)	17	Cleveland	(3.63)
18	Kennedy	(3.60)	18	Taft	(3.90)
19	McKinley	(3.63)		Van Buren	(3.90)
20	Taft	(3.72)	20	McKinley	(3.91)
21	Van Buren	(4.02)	21	Hoover	(4.12)
22	Hayes	(4.04)	22	Hayes	(4.16)
23	Ford	(4.12)	23	Carter	(4.20)
24	Arthur	(4.22)	24	Arthur	(4.33)
25	Coolidge	(4.24)	25	Ford	(4.41)
	Harrison	(4.24)	26	Taylor	(4.43)
27	Taylor	(4.43)	27	Harrison	(4.49)
	Fillmore	(4.34)	28	Fillmore	(4.67)
29	Tyler	(4.44)	29	Tyler	(4.71)
30	Carter	(4.58)	30	Coolidge	(4.79)
31	Nixon	(4.72)	31	Pierce	(5.01)
32	Pierce	(4.76)	32	Buchanan	(5.18)
33	A. Johnson	(4.94)	33	A. Johnson	(5.25)
34	Buchanan	(5.02)	34	Grant	(5.27)
35	Grant	(5.22)	35	Nixon	(5.38)
36	Harding	(5.42)	36	Harding	(5.58)

Note: In terms of methodology, some caution should be observed when using this
table. The Murray-Blessing survey was not designed specifically to analyze
certain very basic personal beliefs held by historians, and we do not believe
that anything but the simple analysis supplied here should be implied or
inferred from our data. The question of the interplay of personal beliefs and
historical analysis demands much more direct examination than is afforded by
our survey.

Appendix 12

First, in order to assure that the returns have not been accidentally biased
in some sense, would you please take a moment and fill in the following
demographic data.

Year of birth: 19_____   Male_____   Female_____   State where born _____

School from which Ph.D. received:_____

Major area and period of teaching and/or research specialty (check only one in
column A and only one in column B)

COLUMN A   COLUMN B (cont.)

_____ Colonial and Revolutionary   _____ U.S. Diplomatic
_____ National Period   _____ U.S. Economic
_____ Middle Period   _____ U.S. Intellectual
_____ Civil War and Reconstruction   _____ U.S. Legal and
_____ U.S. 1877-1900   Constitutional
_____ U.S. 1900-1945   _____ Southern
_____ U.S. since 1945   _____ Western and Frontier
                                                 _____ State and Local
                                                 _____ Immigration and Ethnic
                                                 _____ Other (specify)

COLUMN B
                                                 __ _____

_____ Urban and Quantitative
_____ Afro-American
_____ American Indian
_____ Women's History
_____ U.S. Military
_____ U.S. Political
_____ U.S. Cultural and Social

    Now, please go to the next page to start the survey. Follow the
instructions for each question and, if you should have a question about
anything in the survey, please do not hesitate to call me at (215) 320-4871.

                         Thank you,

                         Tim H. Blessing

Survey Questions - Ronald Reagan's Presidency

1.   In terms of Supreme Court appointments, rate the following "Reagan
      justices" from 1 to 6, 1 being excellent, 6 being poor.

                 3.27 a. Sandra O'Connor
                 3.90 b. Anthony Scalia
                 3.80 c. Arthur Kennedy
                 4.10 d. The appointment of William Rehnquist to the Chief
                         Justiceship.

2.   Do you believe that in the air traffic controllers strike (the PATCO
      strike) Reagan (check one):

      24.4 1. was acting within his rights and the country's best overall
               interests in firing the controllers.
      62.6 2. was acting within his rights but not in the country's best
               overall interests in firing the controllers.
      13.0 3. was not acting within his rights in firing the controllers

3.   Do you believe that Reagan was sincere in his support for the "Moral
      Right?" (Pro-life, prayer in schools, and so on.) (Check one)

      yes, very 13.7   27.4   21.8   8.1   13.7   15.3 no, not sincere
      sincere   1   2   3   4   5   6   at all

4.   Reagan, in sending arms to Afghanistan: (Check one)

      10.4 1. should be credited highly for encouraging the Soviet withdrawal
      28.0 2. should be credited somewhat for encouraging the Soviet
              withdrawal
      48.0 3. had only a limited effect on the withdrawal of the Soviets
      13.6 4. had practically no effect on the withdrawal of the Soviets

5.   Reagan, in terms of his support for few restrictions on firearms: (check
      one)

      63.5 1. was basically wrong and caused the country serious harm
      24.6 2. was basically wrong but really did not cause the country great
              harm
       7.9 3. was basically right, even though more restrictions should have
              been considered
       4.0 4. was basically right

6.   Would you say that in general, during the Reagan years, the morale of
      the American people (check one)

      improved 13.4   52.8   13.4   9.4   8.7   2.4 declined
                  1   2   3   4   5   6

7.   How much of the decline or improvement in the country's overall morale
      would you attribute to Reagan's influence? (check one)

      a great deal 14.2   46.5   19.7   11.6   4.7   3.9 very little
                      1   2   3   4   5   6

8.   In the South Korean passage from military rule to a more democratic
      government, do you believe the Reagan administration (check one)

      36.9 a. gave too little help to the forces of democracy

Survey Questions - Ronald Reagan   page 3

     20.5 b. should have stayed out of the situation altogether
     42.6 c. steered a prudent course in a difficult situation

9.   Overall, during the Reagan years, in regard to the racial policies of
     the South African government: (check one)

     69.6 a. the U.S. should have pushed harder to end apartheid
     11.2 b. the United States should not intentionally interfere in the
           internal affairs of South Africa
     19.2 c. the U.S. steered a prudent course in a difficult situation

10.   Do you believe that welfare and social programs were, in general, during
     the Reagan years: (check one)

     88.7 a. underfunded   2.4 b. overfunded   8.9 c. funded at near the
                                                  proper level

11.   Concerning Israel, would you rank Reagan as (check one)

     60.8 a. a strong supporter of Israel   39.2 b. a lukewarm supporter of
                                                    Israel
     --- c. not a supporter of Israel

12.   Concerning the stock crash of 1987: (check one)

     56.0 a. Reagan's own policies contributed greatly
      .8 b. Reagan simply inherited bad policies
     43.2 c. situations having little to do with governmental policies
           overwhelmed governmental safeguards

13.   How much did Reagan contribute to overcoming the stock crash?

     6.5 a. very much   21.1 b. some   72.4 c. very little

14.   In terms of the press, many conservatives say the press mounted savage
     and biased attacks on Mr. Reagan, while some liberals see the press as
     being seduced, conned, and manipulated by the administration. Was Mr.
     Reagan (check one):

1.6 a. treated too harshly by the press   24.8 b. treated fairly by the press
73.6 c. treated too leniently by the press
15.   Do you consider the Strategic Defense Initiative (check A or B)

    18.3 A. A good idea and (check one)
         31.8 a) we should move toward full development
         22.7 b) we should only go to actual testing
         45.4 c) we should only go to laboratory testing

    81.7 B. A bad idea because of (check as many as apply)
         91.7 a) costs
         47.8 b) strategic implications
         62.1 c) difficulty in achieving a workable system
         4.5 d) other _____

16.   Was Reagan (check one)

     16.1 a. mostly an idealist
     64.4 b. a blender of idealism and pragmatism
     19.5 c. mostly a pragmatist

17.   Concerning relationships with Libya, in general, do you believe that the

Survey Questions - Ronald Reagan   page 4

continued state of tension between Libya and the U.S. is: (check one)

<u>40.8</u> a. mostly Libya's fault   <u>9.6</u> c. mostly the U.S.'s fault
<u>49.6</u> b. caused about equally by both sides

18.   With the exception of the Reykjavik summit, would you say that the other
       Reagan/Gorbachev summits (check one)

<u>42.1</u> a. should be considered a credit   <u>7.1</u> b. should be considered a
         to Reagan   liability to Reagan
<u>50.8</u> c. were really too mixed to assess

19.   At the Reykjavik summit, should Reagan have accepted Gorbachev's offer
       of a grand settlement? (check one)

       <u>40.0</u> a. yes   <u>29.6</u> b. no   <u>30.4</u> c. unsure

20.   During the Reagan years, the economy underwent one of the longest
       sustained advances on record. How much credit do you believe Reagan
       should receive for the advance? (check one)

       <u>16.8</u> a. a great deal <u>48.0</u> b. some <u>35.2</u> c. very little

21.   Under Ronald Reagan, the office of the Presidency became (check one)

much stronger than   <u>5.7</u> <u>29.3</u> <u>39.0</u> <u>17.9</u> <u>6.5</u> <u>1.6</u>   much weaker than
it had been   1   2   3   4   5   6   it had been

22.   Do you believe that budget deficit is a serious danger to the country?
       (check one)

       <u>86.6</u> a. yes   <u>1.6</u> b. no   <u>11.8</u> c. unsure
23.   Regardless of your answer to #22, who, during the Reagan years, do you
       believe has been most at fault for the deficit? (check one)

<u>70.5</u> a. the president <u>15.6</u> b. the Congress <u>13.9</u> c. the inherited situation

24.   Did Reagan pursue the correct course in sending ships to patrol the
       Persian Gulf? (check one)

       <u>.8</u> a. Yes, but we should have been more willing to commit to action
       <u>42.7</u> b. Yes, and we mostly followed the proper balance between action
            and restraint
       <u>21.8</u> c. Yes, but we were too ready to commit to action
       <u>34.7</u> d. No, we should not have been there

25.   Under Reagan, inheritance taxes were cut. Was this a good idea? (check
       one)

       <u>22.8</u> a. yes   <u>56.7</u> b. no   <u>20.5</u> c. unsure

26.   Did Reagan do as much as he should have to help the farmers?

       <u>19.8</u> a. yes   <u>57.1</u> b. no   <u>23.0</u> c. unsure

27.   Was Reagan right in his judgement that the courts have now arrogated to
       themselves too many powers over too many things? (check one)

              Yes <u>10.7</u> <u>11.6</u> <u>5.8</u>   <u>11.6</u> <u>34.7</u> <u>25.6</u> No
                    1   2   3   4   5   6

28.   Should Reagan have done much more to obtain the release of the hostages

Survey Questions - Ronald Reagan   page 5

in Lebanon? (check one)

34.7 a. No, there was little he could do without unacceptable risks to
        the hostages
41.1 b. No, even if there were more things which could have been done,
        they would have been too likely to compromise the U.S.'s
        position on hostage-taking
 6.5 c. Yes, even to the point of force
 7.3 d. Yes, he should have tried to deal with the Moslem extremists,
        even at the cost of national honor
 9.7 e. Other (specify)

29.   The farmer has had a very difficult time over the last decade. Is this
      more the result of

      26.4 a. the situation Reagan inherited
      24.8 b. the Reagan administration's handling of the problem
      36.4 c. the result of outside forces
      12.4 d. not sure

30.   How would you rate the Reagan administration's overall involvement in
      the transfer of power from Marcos to Aquino?

              High 11.1   26.2   27.0   15.1   14.3   6.3 Low
                    1   2   3   4   5   6

31.   Did the Reagan administration have a major role in continuing Marcos'
      long exercise of power?

              Yes 27.8   40.5   13.5   9.5   7.1   1.6 No
                   1   2   3   4   5   6

32.   Was the Reagan administration sufficiently supportive of the Aquino
      regime, once it was established?

              Yes 13.5   42.1   22.7   9.5   7.1   5.6 No
                   1   2   3   4   5   6

33.   Was Reagan right in his judgement that recent Congresses have almost
      always spent more than has been prudent? (check one)

              Yes 18.9   17.3   14.2   12.6   24.4   12.6 No
                   1   2   3   4   5   6

34.   Did the United States have adequate reasons, in terms of American lives
      and property, to invade Grenada? (check one)

              15.3 a. yes   84.7 b. no

36.   In terms of crises both domestic and foreign, regardless of how they
      were resolved, would you say that, overall, Reagan faced: (check one)

 .8 a. a very large number   4.7 b. a large number   56.7 c. an average
                                                                   number
26.0 d. a below average number   11.8 e. a small number

37.   Regardless of his own actions, do you believe that Reagan was right in
      saying that the Federal government has become dangerously unresponsive
      to the people?

Survey Questions - Ronald Reagan   page 6

Yes <u>10.5</u> <u>27.4</u> <u>21.0</u> <u>11.3</u> <u>17.7</u> <u>12.1</u> No
    1   2   3   4   5   6

38.   Do you think that Reagan was too attentive to the "Moral
      Right?"
                Yes <u>40.0</u> <u>29.6</u> <u>15.2</u> <u>9.6</u> <u>4.8</u> <u>.6</u> No
                    1   2   3   4   5   6

39.   Rate from 1-6 (1 being extremely serious and 6 being not serious at all)
      the threat to American constitutional processes and guaranties in the
      following uses of Presidential power.

<u>2.13</u> a. Andrew Jackson's refusal to follow the Supreme Court on Indian Removal
<u>2.75</u> b. Cleveland's use of federal power to break the Pullman Strike
<u>2.98</u> c. T. Roosevelt's aid to the Panamanian Rebels
<u>2.41</u> d. Wilson's restriction of personal liberties in World War I
<u>3.08</u> e. Hoover's use of force on the "bonus army"
<u>2.98</u> f. F. Roosevelt's attempt to pack the Supreme Court
<u>2.05</u> g. Lyndon Johnson's use of executive power in Vietnam
<u>1.68</u> h. Nixon and the events collected under the term Watergate
<u>2.07</u> i. The Iran-Contra Affair under Reagan

40.   Do you believe the tax reform act of 1986 should be counted, for
      President Reagan, as (check one)

      <u>17.4</u> a. an asset   <u>35.5</u> b. a liability   <u>47.1</u> c. neither

41.   Regardless of your answer to the above, did the tax reform act of 1986
      improve the tax structure? (check one)

            <u>27.4</u> a. yes   <u>49.2</u> b. no   <u>23.4</u> c. unsure

42.   The United States should have promoted the transfer from military rule
      to a more democratic government in Chile: (check one)

      <u>51.6</u> a. more vigorously
      <u>11.9</u> b. about the same
      <u>36.5</u> c. less vigorously
      <u>   </u> d. The United States should not intentionally interfere in the
               internal affairs of Chile.

43.   Do you believe the trade imbalance is a serious danger to the country?
      (check one)

      <u>83.5</u> a. yes   <u>4.7</u> b. no   <u>11.8</u> c. unsure

44.   Regardless of your answer to #43, who, during the Reagan years, do you
      believe has been more at fault for the continuing trade imbalance?

      <u>66.3</u> a. the President <u>19.8</u> b. the Congress   <u>13.9</u> c. other forces

45.   Do you believe Mr. Reagan had a significant influence on the conditions
      leading to the 1989 political changes in eastern Europe? (check one)

      <u>51.6</u> a. yes   <u>49.0</u> b. no

Survey Questions - Ronald Reagan   page 7

46.   How much credit should the Reagan administration receive for the INF
      treaty? (check one)

      a good   13.6 27.1 37.3   9.3 10.2   2.5 very little
      deal   1   2   3   4   5   6

47.   Should the president have gone to Bitburg? (check one)

            12.1 a. yes   87.9 b. no

48.   Would you say that, leaving aside the Iran-contra affair, Mr. Reagan
      should have tried to open some lines of communication with Iranian
      leaders?

            84.0 a. yes   16.0 b. no

Optional Comment:

49.   Regardless of his own actions, was Reagan right in believing the Federal
      government has become dangerously intrusive?

            Yes 6.3 22.2 18.3 14.3 24.6 14.3 No
                   1   2   3   4   5   6

50.   Your overall evaluation of Nancy Reagan is (check one)

            .8 a. very positive   4.8 b. positive   16.0 c. neutral
          41.6 d. negative   36.8 e. very negative

Optional Comment

51.   Was Reagan's view that the Sandinistas were a serious threat to the
      stability of Central America (check one)

      mostly right 4.0 12.7 10.3 14.3 26.2 32.5 mostly wrong
                      1   2   3   4   5   6

52.   Was the Reagan tax cut of 1981 basically a good idea? (check one)

      definitely 5.6   8.0   8.8 15.2 21.6 40.6 definitely not
                    1   2   3   4   5   6

53.   Should the United States have promoted the cause of Solidarity in
      Poland?

18.7 a. more vigorously   54.5 b. about the same   .8 c. less vigorously
26.0 d. the United States should not intentionally be involved with Poland's
        internal affairs
54.   How, in terms of taxation, would you evaluate the following groups' tax
      burdens before the 1981 tax cut (check the appropriate lines)

	undertaxed	overtaxed	appropriately taxed
a. The lower socio-economic groups	3.3	69.2	27.5
b. The middle socio-economic groups	3.3	61.7	35.0
c. The upper socio-economic groups	85.8	3.3	10.8
d. Businesses	63.9	6.7	29.4

Survey Questions - Ronald Reagan   page 8

55.   The Reagan administration's belief that the existing public housing
       programs are generally "disastrous:"

       _72.4_ a. was basically right   _27.6_ b. was basically wrong

56.   Concerning public housing (and regardless of your answer to #55), should
       Reagan have (check one)

       _77.4_ a. budgeted more money for public housing
       _10.5_ b. budgeted less money for public housing
       _12.1_ c. budgeted about the same amount for public housing

57.   Given that both have their strengths and weaknesses, which, <u>over the
       long haul of the presidency</u>, (hence for presidents in general), is the
       better style: (check one)

       _64.7_ a. The Reagan tendency to delegate authority, with the president
                  sticking mostly to policy.
       _34.5_ b. The Carter style of intense involvement in many of the details of
                  executive administration.

58.   Was Reagan right in asking the courts to apply a stricter construction
       to the constitution?

                 Yes _11.9_ _9.5_ _8.7_ _12.7_ _29.4_ _27.8_ No
                       1   2   3   4   5   6

59.   In regard to the Iran/Contra affair, do you believe Reagan realized that
       he was swapping arms for hostages? (check one)

_76.2_ a. yes   _16.7_ b. no
 _7.1_ c. Other (specify)

60.   Do you believe that Reagan knew that money from Iran was flowing to the
       Contras?

       _84.8_ a. Yes   _81.1_ b. No

        _7.2_ c. Other (specify)

61.   During the Reagan years, should the United States have promoted the
       cause of the environment in Brazil:

_76.0_ a. more vigorously
_13.2_ b. about the same
_----_ c. less vigorously
_10.7_ d. the United States should not intervene in the internal affairs of
           other countries.

62.   Rate the funding levels of the following welfare and social programs
       under Reagan:

	overfunded	funded appropriately	underfunded	unsure
Social Security	_26.0_	_57.7_	_13.8_	_2.4_
Medicare	_4.7_	_37.8_	_54.3_	_3.1_
Student Loans	_3.1_	_21.3_	_70.9_	_4.7_

Survey Questions - Ronald Reagan   page   9

Women's Programs	10.2	18.1	55.1	16.5
Aid to Secondary Education	3.1	21.3	71.7	3.9
Aid to Minorities (including set-asides)	7.9	15.7	66.1	10.2

63.   How much of the 1981-1982 recession was attributable to Reagan's economic policies? (check one)

    most 15.2   25.6   17.6   13.6   20.0   8.0   very little
            1   2   3   4   5   6

64.   How should Reagan have regarded the request of the Caribbean leaders who asked him to intervene in Grenada?

12.3 a. as requests which, once made, could not be ignored without seriously damaging America's credibility;
47.5 b. as requests which, once made, could have been turned down with only a small loss of credibility.
39.3 c. as requests which, once made, could have been ignored with practically no loss to American credibility.

65.   Do you believe that the Reagan administration influence over events in the Middle East (check one)

14.4 a. was about as much as could be expected given the situation
51.2 b. reflects a record of ineptitude
34.4 c. can be considered to be neither a disaster nor a success

66.   Do you believe that Reagan's calls for long prison terms for violent and habitual criminals (check one)

42.5 1. should be an integral part of programs to stop crime
33.1 2. should be considered at least as a useful temporary expedient
18.1 3. should be considered as misguided
6.3   4. have been actually harmful

67.   Were the Reagan plans for an enlarged navy

6.4   1. a good idea
6.4   2. a good idea, but too expensive
9.6   3. a good idea, but not well-planned
15.2 4. both 2 & 3
62.4 5. not a good idea

68.   Was the Reagan administration correct in opening talks with the PLO? (check one).

    90.5 a. yes   2.4 b. no   7.1 c. unsure

69.   Was President Reagan too tolerant of Israel's occasional military incursions against its neighbors? (check one)

    77.8 a. yes   15.1 b. no   7.1 c. unsure

70.   Do you believe that the economic advance was confined only to the top sectors of society? (check one)

    65.6 a. yes   11.2 b. no, there was some   23.2 c. no, most (but
                               advance in all parts   not all) of

Survey Questions - Ronald Reagan   page 10

                        of society   society joined
                                                                            in

71.   What role do you believe Nancy Reagan played in the Reagan Presidency?

  .8 a.   She was more in charge than Reagan
15.6 b.   She was more influential than any other advisor
46.7 c.   She was more influential than many of Reagan's senior advisors
28.7 d.   She had real influence, but less than the senior advisors
 7.4 e.   She had only moderate influence
  .8 f.   She had little influence

Optional Comment:

72.   In terms of national security, was it in America's best interests to
      invade Grenada? (check one)

       19.2 a. yes   80.8 b. no
73.   Evaluate Reagan's qualifications for the presidency in 1980. Would you
      say that in terms of background and intellect

       7.3 a.   he was well qualified in both background and intellect
      37.9 b.   he was well qualified in background but not intellect
      ---- c.   he was well qualified in intellect but not background
      54.0 d.   he was not qualified in either background or intellect

74.   Some analysts see Reagan's military buildup as having created pressures
      which played a key role in the change of Russia's military posture. Do
      you (check one)

 9.7 a. believe that the American military buildup did play a key role
38.7 b. believe that the American military buildup had some impact. but was
         not a primary factor
41.1 c. believe that an American military buildup played only a minor role
10.5 d. believe that the American military buildup played no role at all

75.   Should the Reagan administration have continued to keep troops in Korea?
      (check one)

13.0 a. Yes, at the same or higher level
28.5 b. Yes, but at a significantly lower level
42.3 c. Yes, but the Reagan people should have begun a slow movement towards
         eventual total withdrawal
16.3 d. no

76.   How would you rate the Reagan record on terrorism? (check one)

            High .8   6.6   14.8 23.8 32.0 22.1 Low
                  1   2   3   4   5   6

77.   Should the United States have promoted the cause of glasnost and
      perestroika in the Soviet Union? (check one)

25.6 a. more vigorously   50.4 b. about the same   2.4 c. less vigorously
21.5 d. the United States should not become involved with the internal
        affairs of the Soviet Union

78.   Is it possible that most of the "sleaze" in the "sleaze factor" came
      about because the forces outside the oval office are demanding ever

Survey Questions - Ronald Reagan   page 11

higher standards of propriety in office and not because the Reagan
people really differed that much from other administrations:

<u>79.8</u> a. No, the Reagan people really were <u>more</u> corrupt
<u>8.1</u> b. Yes, the Reagan people simply were caught by a tide of rising
              expectations
<u>12.1</u> c. Unsure

79.   Did the Reagan administration handle negotiations with the Soviets on
       disarmament and disengagement well?

<u>8.0</u> a. yes, very well   <u>48.0</u> b. yes, well   <u>37.6</u> c. no, not well
<u>6.4</u> d. no, not well at all

80.   Do you believe Reagan should have backtracked and raised taxes as the
       budget deficit increased?

<u>82.5</u> a. yes   <u>9.5</u> b. no   <u>7.9</u> c. unsure

81.   Do you agree with Reagan's remarks at Bitburg that the soldiers who died
       for the Third Reich were victims of tyranny just as those who died in
       the Holocaust?

<u>18.9</u> a. yes   <u>81.1</u> b. no

82.   How aware do you believe Mr. Reagan was concerning William Casey's
       attempt to build a CIA which could operate independently of Congress?

quite aware <u>24.0</u> <u>32.8</u> <u>20.8</u> <u>9.6</u> <u>10.4</u> <u>2.4</u> quite unaware
              1   2   3   4   5   6

83.   Do you believe that the American attempt to impose order in Beirut was
       (check one)

<u>12.1</u> a. a good idea, but flawed in execution
<u>18.5</u> b. a good idea, ruined, less by bad execution than by the
              difficulties inherent in trying to stop true fanatics
<u>69.4</u> c. not a good idea

84.   Regardless of his own actions, was Reagan right in saying that more
       powers should be transferred back from the Federal government to state
       and local governments?

Yes <u>10.2</u> <u>11.8</u> <u>23.6</u> <u>15.0</u> <u>18.1</u> <u>21.3</u> No
       1   2   3   4   5   6

85.   Which statement best fits Reagan in terms of environmental issues?

<u>90.4</u> a. Too inattentive to environmental concerns
<u>3.2</u> b. He tried to maintain a balance between environmental concerns and
              economic concerns
<u>6.4</u> c. Too inattentive to economic concerns in relation to the environment

Survey Questions - Ronald Reagan   page 12

86.   After the indictment of Noriega, should Reagan have

12.3 a. used direct force if necessary to remove Noriega
---- b. blockaded Panama if necessary to remove Noriega
10.7 c. used even sterner economic measures to remove Noriega
30.3 d. refused to become involved with Panama's internal crisis, regardless
         of opportunity
42.6 e. in reality, there were few viable options for handling Noriega
 4.1 f. Other (specify)

87.   Has the Reagan defensive build-up helped the United States's
       conventional ground forces:

       greatly .9   14.7 30.2 19.8 25.0   9.5 not at all
                 1   2   3   4   5   6

88.   Overall, but excluding the Strategic Defense Initiative, would you say
       that you see the military buildup as:

 1.6 a. not enough
 8.9 b. about enough
24.2 c. somewhat too much
45.2 d. much too much
20.2 e. totally unnecessary

89.   If the weapons and supplies used by the armed services could be secured
       more efficiently than they are now, would you:

 4.1 1. support more of a military buildup
95.9 2. have the same feelings about a military buildup as expressed in
         Question #88

90.   In terms of issues avoided, would you say that the Reagan administration
       avoided

38.4 a. a very large number
36.8 b, a large number
24.0 c. an average number
---- d. a below average number
  .8 e. a small number

91.   Should Reagan have held more news conferences?

       65.5 a. yes   34.5 b. no

92.   Reagan has often been criticized as being too loyal to unworthy
       subordinates. Did this trait: (check the one which most applies)

86.3 a. hurt his administration more than it helped
 2.4 b. help his administration more than it hurt
11.3 c. This is an inaccurate characterization.

93.   In terms of creating a body of homeless, how much blame do you attach to
       the Reagan administration?

Survey Questions - Ronald Reagan   page 13

    a great deal <u>33.1</u> <u>32.3</u> <u>16.5</u> <u>4.7</u> <u>10.2</u> <u>3.1</u> very little
                    1   2   3   4   5   6

94.   In terms of helping the homeless, <u>should</u> the Reagan administration have done?

    much more <u>55.1</u> <u>26.8</u> <u>11.8</u> <u>1.6</u> <u>2.4</u> <u>2.1</u> very little more
               1   2   3   4   5   6

95. In terms of human rights in the Soviet Union:

<u> 5.7 </u> a. Reagan risked too much with his public displays for human rights
<u>24.4</u> b. Reagan should have pushed even harder for human rights
<u>44.7</u> c. Reagan steered a prudent course in a difficult situation
<u>25.2</u> d. The U.S. should not get involved in the internal affairs of the
          Soviet Union.

96. In terms of the Equal Rights Amendment:

<u>22.4</u> a. Reagan was essentially right in objecting to it
<u>58.4</u> b. Reagan should have fallen in behind it and pushed for it
<u>16.0</u> c. Reagan should have kept his objections private and allowed state
          legislators to decide without knowing the President's wishes.
<u> 3.2 </u> d. Other (specify)

97.   On balance, should Reagan have asked the U.S.'s Allies to pay more of their defense costs?

          <u>99.2</u> a. Yes   <u>.8</u> b. No

98.   On matters of race, would you describe the Reagan administration as being (check one)

<u>27.9</u> a. very racist
<u>38.5</u> b. somewhat racist
<u>18.9</u> c. mildly racist
<u>14.8</u> d. reasonably evenhanded
99.   How would you rank the Reagan administration's overall dealings with:

Panama?   High <u> .8 </u> <u>4.1</u> <u>12.2</u> <u>17.1</u> <u>24.4</u> <u>41.5</u> Low
                         1   2   3   4   5   6

El Salvador?   High <u>----</u> <u>1.6</u> <u>8.2</u> <u>15.6</u> <u>29.5</u> <u>45.1</u> Low
                         1   2   3   4   5   6

Mexico?   High <u>----</u> <u>8.2</u> <u>17.2</u> <u>43.4</u> <u>23.0</u> <u>8.2</u> Low
                         1   2   3   4   5   6

100. Did Reagan distrust the Soviet Union too much?

         Yes <u>26.2</u> <u>32.8</u> <u>12.3</u> <u>9.0</u> <u>11.5</u> <u>8.2</u> No
             1   2   3   4   5   6

101. Do you believe that Reagan was right to ask to have Roe vs. Wade overturned so that the issue of abortion could be settled at the state level? (check one)

Survey Questions - Ronald Reagan   page 14

       22.0 a. Yes   77.2 b. No

102. Do you believe that Robert Bork (check one):

18.5 a. was well-qualified in terms of judicial and legal expertise and
         should have been seated
57.3 b. was well-qualified in terms of judicial and legal expertise, but
         should not have been seated
24.2 c. was not well-qualified

103. Concerning the bombing of Libya, do you believe that this was

15.4 a. a lawful response and in the nation's best interest.
 7.3 b. a lawful response, but not in the nation's best interest.
14.6 c. an unlawful response, but still in the nations's best interest.
62.6 d. an unlawful response and not in the nation's best interest.

104. In terms of pure leadership -- that is getting people to follow him
      where he wanted to go -- Mr. Reagan should rank

23.6 a. very highly 45.5 b. high 21.1 c. average   9.8 d. not very
high

105. Would it have been in the United States' best interest to have promoted
      the cause of land reform more vigorously in Central America?

79.7 a. yes
 4.1 b. no
16.3 c. the United States should not interfere in Central America's internal
         affairs

106. Was Reagan right in regarding the stability of the South African
government as being more in the United States' national interest than
the internal racial policies of South Africa?

      definitely 4.0   4.8   8.8 16.8 33.6   32.0 definitely not
                   1   2   3   4   5   6

107. In relation to the Contras of Nicaragua, the Reagan administration (with
      the exception of the Iran-Contra affair) should be (check the
      appropriate response)

      praised for   3.2   4.0   4.8 11.3   21.8 54.8   condemned for its
      its support   1   2   3   4   5   6   support

108. Do you believe that Reagan's calls for long prison terms for "kingpins"
      in the drug trade

50.4 a. should be an integral part of programs to stop drug trafficking
32.5 b. should be considered at least as a useful temporary expedient
12.2 c. should be considered as misguided
 4.9 d. were actually harmful

109. How much of the Soviet movement toward disengagement do you attribute to
      Reagan's stands on matters of disarmament?

 8.1 a. highly significant   18.5 b. significant amount   66.9 c. small
      amount   amount
 6.5 d. not at all

110. Given the high approval ratings shown for Mr. Reagan in public opinion
      polls, would you say that:

Survey Questions - Ronald Reagan   page 15

91.8 a. the American people have overestimated Mr. Reagan
 8.2 b. the American people have judged Mr. Reagan correctly

111. On matters of gender, would you describe the Reagan administration as
      being

32.8 a. very sexist   40.0 b. somewhat sexist   16.0 c. mildly sexist
11.2 d. fairly evenhanded

112. Can the PLO be trusted at this time?

16.3 a. yes   26.8 b. no   56.9 c. unsure

113. Was the Soviet Union an "evil empire"

      Under Stalin?   Yes 56.6 23.8 4.9 3.3 2.5 9.0 No
                                1   2   3   4   5   6

114. Under Khrushchev?   Yes 8.2 15.6 22.0 23.8 11.5 13.9 No
                               1   2   3   4   5   6

115. Under Brezhnev?   Yes 6.6 26.2 26.2 21.3 4.1 15.6 No
                               1   2   3   4   5   6

116. On a scale of one to six, one being most corrupt and six being least
      corrupt, and in the light of other administrations, how corrupt would
      you consider the following administrations?

      Grant 2.22   Truman 3.73   Nixon 2.35

      Harrison 3.79   Eisenhower 3.97   Reagan 2.52

      Harding 2.23   L. Johnson 3.82   Kennedy 4.25

117. On a scale of one to six, one being most imperial, six being least
      imperial, how would you rate the following administrations:

      F. Roosevelt 2.57   Kennedy   2.74   Ford   4.17

      Truman 3.26   L. Johnson 2.05   Carter 4.62

      Eisenhower 3.57   Nixon 2.00   Reagan 2.62

118. The effect which Reagan had on the nation's value systems was (check
      one)

      14.4 a. was significant and positive
      68.0 b. was significant and negative
      17.6 c. was insignificant

119. In terms of his legislative program, Reagan left behind (check one)

      17.5 a) a large legacy
      36.5 b) a moderate legacy
      44.4 c) a small legacy

Survey Questions - Ronald Reagan   page 16

120. In terms of party leadership, Reagan

     29.8 a) was a strong party leader
     26.6 b) was a weak party leader
     43.5 c) was a moderate party leader

121. Reagan controlled the agenda of the country's political life (check one)

     12.8 a) only weakly
     43.2 b) moderately
     44.0 c) strongly

122. Would you judge Ronald Reagan's personal integrity to be (check one)

     15.4 a) high
     52.8 b) average
     31.7 c) low

123. Which do you believe most influenced Americans to elect and re-elect Mr.
      Reagan? (check one)

     60.3 a. his personal attributes
      4.1 b. his proposed policies
     35.5 c. the weakness of his Democratic opponents

124. If you could sum up Reagan, the president, in four adjectives or
      adjective phrases, what would they be?

      1. _____   2. _____

      3. _____   4. _____

125. If you could sum up Reagan, the person, in four adjectives or
      adjective phrases, what would they be?

1. _____
2. _____
3. _____
4. _____

(Please go to the next page.)

Using the following Schlesinger categories, rate Reagan as president as

Survey Questions - Ronald Reagan   page 17

    (Check one)

Great	Near Great	Above Average	Average	Below Average	Failure
2.1	2.4	17.3	21.5	43.4	13.2

Optional Comments:

Notes

INTRODUCTION

1. Richard E. Neustadt, *Presidential Power: The Politics of Leadership, with Reflections on Johnson and Nixon* (New York: Wiley and Son, 1976), p. 185.

2. Sidney Hyman, "The Qualities That Make a President," *New York Times Magazine*, December 1, 1963, p. 23.

3. Neustadt, *Presidential Power*, p. 35.

4. Clinton Rossiter, *The American Presidency*, rev. ed. (New York: Harcourt Brace and World, 1960), pp. 15–16, 108.

5. Such studies include Gary M. Maranell, "The Evaluation of Presidents: An Extension of the Schlesinger Polls," *Journal of American History*, vol. 57, no. 1 (June 1970), pp. 104–113; Dean Keith Simonton, "Presidential Greatness and Performance: Can We Predict Leadership in the White House?" *Journal of Personality*, vol. 49, no. 3 (September 1981), pp. 306–323; H. W. Wendt and P. C. Light, "Measuring 'Greatness' in American Presidents: Model Case of International Research on Political Leadership?" *European Journal of Social Psychology*, vol. 6 (1976), pp. 105–109; Thomas E. Kynerd, "An Analysis of Presidential Greatness and 'President Rating,' " *Southern Quarterly*, vol. 9 (1971), pp. 304–329. Political science professor James David Barber has also worked in this general field of assessing presidential leadership and character.

6. Kristen Monroe, *Presidential Popularity and the Economy* (New York: Praeger Publishers, 1984).

7. Ibid., pp. 162, 174–183, 187–204.

8. George C. Edwards III and Stephen J. Wayne, *Presidential Leadership: Politics and Policy Making* (New York: St. Martin's Press, 1985); George C. Edwards III and Stephen J. Wayne, eds., *Studying the Presidency* (Knoxville: University of Tennessee Press, 1983).

9. In recent years, there has been a growing minority of American historians who see limitations in this "presidential synthesis" view of American history and have seriously sought an end to it.

10. See the examples already cited in note 5 above.

11. Thomas E. Cronin, *The State of the Presidency* (Boston: Little, Brown and Co., 1975), p. 10, quoting Cochran.

CHAPTER 1

1. Only the polls involving the rating of presidents by professional historians concern us here.

2. *Life*, November 1, 1948, pp. 65–66, 68, 73–74.

3. This poll also included one Supreme Court Justice (Felix Frankfurter) and three Britishers (one being Denis W. Brogan).

4. Arthur M. Schlesinger, Sr., "Our Presidents: A Rating by 75 Historians," *New York Times Magazine*, July 29, 1962, pp. 12–13, 40–41, 43.

5. Thomas A. Bailey, *Presidential Greatness: The Image and the Man from George Washington to the Present* (New York: Appleton-Century, 1966), p. 24, quoting Schlesinger's instructions.

6. Ibid., pp. 25–28, 31–33.

7. Ibid., pp. 252–266.

8. For Bailey's own evaluation of the presidents, see ibid., pp. 267–335.

9. For a description of this poll and comments on it, see *Parade*, May 8, 1977, pp. 16, 19. See also Robert E. DiClerico, *The American President* (New York: Prentice-Hall, 1979), p. 332.

10. An original copy of the Porter poll is in the possession of Robert K. Murray, who was a participant. The results have recently appeared in print in William D. Pederson and Ann M. McLaurin, eds., *The Rating Game in American Politics* (New York: Irvington Publishers, 1987), p. 33.

11. The four historians who also took part in the original Schlesinger survey were Marcus Cunliffe, David H. Donald, Dumas Malone, and Earl Pomeroy.

12. Steve Neal, "Our Best and Worst Presidents," *Chicago Tribune Magazine*, January 10, 1982, pp. 8–13, 15, 18.

CHAPTER 2

1. American Historical Association, *Guide to Departments of History, 1979–80* (Washington, D.C.: AHA, 1979); American Historical Association *Guide to Departments of History, 1980–81* (Washington D.C.: AHA, 1980).

2. For the basic rules and studies concerning mail surveys, see Paul L. Erdos, *Professional Mail Surveys*, 2nd ed. (Malabar, Fla.: Robert E. Krieger Publishing, 1983), p. 144, and Don A. Dillman, *Mail and Telephone Surveys* (New York: John Wiley and Sons, 1978), p. 55.

3. Both the test poll and the personal interviews indicated that historians were divided over the use of computers and statistical studies in history. Only about 30 percent *readily* accepted computers and statistical devices. All test poll results and material from the oral interviews are held by Tim H. Blessing. All returned mail questionnaires are in the possession of Robert K. Murray.

4. Portions of the remaining material in this chapter first appeared in Robert K. Murray and Tim H. Blessing, "The Presidential Performance Study: A Progress Report," *Journal of American History*, vol. 70, no. 3 (December 1983), pp. 535–555.

5. Birth states having between twenty and fifty respondents were Texas (45), Pennsylvania (44), California (41), New Jersey (39), Iowa (35), Missouri (28), Indiana (27), Minnesota (24), Massachusetts (20), and Wisconsin (20).

6. Other subject specialties were southern (55), western and frontier (48), economic (46), legal and constitutional (40), military (34), Afro-American (27), urban and quantitative (23), and state and local (21).

7. Institutions contributing between fifteen and twenty-five Ph.D.'s were the University of Texas (22), University of North Carolina (20), University of Michigan (19), Uni-

versity of Missouri (18), University of Minnesota (17), Ohio State University (15), University of Pennsylvania (15), and Princeton University (15).

8. According to the answers given on their questionnaires, these 846 historians taught slightly more than 200,000 college students per year.

9. These rankings were based on mean averages calculated by assigning a factor of one to the category of Great, two to Near Great, three to Above Average, and so on to six for Failure. This calculation resulted in means that ranged from 1.13 for Lincoln to 5.56 for Harding. The mode (the category designation of a president by the largest number of respondents) was used as the measure for a president's category standing.

10. See the end of Chapter 1 for the anomaly concerning Franklin Roosevelt's precise standing in the *Chicago Tribune* poll. The overall point totals in that poll presaged what the Murray-Blessing results confirmed concerning FDR's second position. A 1977 survey ranking the presidents as moral leaders, given to American Studies professors in both the United States and the United Kingdom, also resulted in Franklin Roosevelt coming in second. See Ronald A. Wells, "American Presidents as Political and Moral Leaders: A Report on Four Surveys," *Fides et Historia*, vol. 11 (Fall 1978), pp. 39–53.

11. For each of these six presidents (Cleveland, Buchanan, Andrew Johnson, Hoover, Wilson, and Truman), an analysis of variance indicated that at least one age-group differed significantly from at least one other age-group in judging the president. Findings for each of these six presidents showed clear and significant trends; comparisons with the findings for other presidents revealed no similar trends for the others. In any case, there was a 95 percent certainty that significant differences existed among certain age-groups in rating the presidents in Appendix 3.

12. As determined by a comparison-of-means test. For those not familiar with the use of significance levels, the lower the level, the more likely some significant difference exists. A .05 level is traditionally considered to be the minimum needed for something to be highly significant. For instance, in Appendix 4 the difference between male and female views of Carter is highly significant, whereas the difference between the evaluations of Grant is only significant.

13. The ranking by historians of presidents in their time-period concentrations were subjected to an analysis of variance test and to the Duncan, Fisher, and Scheffe procedures at a significance level of .05.

14. For each president, each subject specialty was isolated, its mean rating was determined, and then the mean was compared to the mean for all the remaining specialties. A comparison-of-means test was used for the final evaluation. See Appendix 6.

15. In relation to publications, no combining of factors or any test showed any variations among the presidents at the .05 level of significance. On all regressive procedures, publication factors were invariably found to be nonsignificant ($\alpha = .05$). Evaluations of the interactions of publication factors with other independent variables likewise showed little significance, as did visual inspection of scatterplots of publication factors versus standardized rankings of individual presidents.

16. Only when the rankings of those with Ph.D.'s from the Big Ten and those with Ph.D.'s from the Ivy League were compared did any significant differences appear, and these involved only five presidents—Van Buren, Arthur, Hayes, Eisenhower, and Ford.

17. Regressing the scholastic and demographic factors against presidential ratings showed the highest R2 to be Cleveland's .149; all the other presidents had R2 values below .10,

and most were well below .10, as indicated in Appendix 7. This means that less than 15 percent of Cleveland's ranking and less than 10 percent of the rankings of all other presidents can be attributed to demographic and academic variables among the responding historians.

18. We cannot claim to have considered *all* the "human factors" that might enter into an individual historian's response. We did not, for example, ask those surveyed to indicate political party affiliation, income level, race, or religious preference because we feared that to do so would scare off many potential respondents. But on the basis of what we now know about the effects of the other factors, we do not believe that inclusion of this information would have produced significantly different results.

CHAPTER 3

1. One study has claimed a connection between presidential "greatness" and height, but we were unable to validate it. See Simonton, "Presidential Greatness and Performance," p. 313.

2. See Appendix 1, Section II, 7.

3. Appendix 1, Section III, Part A, 35; Part B, 36; Part C, 42.

4. Appendix 1, Section III, Part C, 34.

5. Richard Hofstadter, "The Right Man for the Big Job," *New York Times Magazine*, April 3, 1960, p. 27, quoting Rossiter; Milton Plesur, "The Health of Presidents," in Rexford G. Tugwell and Thomas E. Cronin, eds., *The Presidency Reappraised* (New York: Praeger, 1974), p. 201. Although some of his conclusions are dubious, see also Michael P. Riccards, "The Presidency: In Sickness and in Health," *Presidential Studies Quarterly*, vol. 7, no. 4 (1977), pp. 215–231.

6. See the survey questions in Appendix 1, Section II, 10, 27, 36. For comparisons, see Section III, Part C, 35, 38.

7. Ten presidents were Episcopalians, seven were Presbyterians, two (Hoover and Nixon) were Quakers, one (Kennedy) was Roman Catholic, and the remainder were distributed among the other Protestant faiths. Garfield (who was not ranked) was the only president who was an ordained minister (Church of Christ). Four presidents—Jackson, Pierce, Polk, and Buchanan—joined a church only after leaving the White House. Eisenhower was the only president to move from baptism to communicant standing in a church (Presbyterian) while chief executive.

8. Appendix 1, Section II, 6, 23, 47. Neither the age nor the gender of the respondents showed any significant variations on their replies to these questions concerning religion.

9. Appendix 1, Section II, 1. In connection with presidential birth and family ancestry, one interesting recent quantitative study has claimed that presidents from large families showed more moderation and more poise and polish, and displayed less forcefulness and less inflexibility, than those from small families, and further, that firstborn children among the presidents tended to lack poise and polish as well as intellectual brilliance. See Dean K. Simonton, "Presidential Personality: Biographical Use of the Gough Adjective Check List," *Journal of Personality and Social Psychology*, vol. 51, no. 1 (1986), p. 153.

10. Appendix 1, Section III, Part A, 29.

11. Appendix 1, Section II, 30, 52. Seven percent would countenance no divorces at all.

12. The first evaluation of this "grouping" by collegiate degrees was contained in Arthur

B. Murphy, "Evaluating the Presidents of the United States," p. 14, draft of a paper sent to Robert K. Murray.

13. See Appendix 1, Section II, 9, 33.

14. Appendix 1, Section II, 41, 63.

15. Appendix 1, Section II, 44.

16. Hofstadter, "The Right Man for the Big Job," p. 121.

17. See Appendix 1, Section II, 58.

18. See Appendix 1, Section II, 64.

19. See Appendix 1, Section II, 20.

20. The rating for the four "professional" military men, alone, was somewhat lower— 4.23, but this was still higher than the 4.87 for the "most prepresidential experience" group.

21. Simonton, "Presidential Greatness and Performance," p. 306.

22. The last *sitting* vice-president elected president was Van Buren in 1936. The only two-term *sitting* vice-president elected as president was the nation's first vice-president, John Adams, who succeeded Washington.

23. See also Appendix 1, Section III, Part A, 35; Section III, Part B, 36; and Section III, Part C, 42.

24. See Appendix 1, Section III, Part A, 22; Section III, Part B, 16, 30; Section III, Part C, 7, 38. See also Section III, Part C, 13 and 18.

25. CBS News Special, "Five Presidents on the Presidency," (1970), with Eric Sevareid (rerun on PBS with Bill Moyer, September 8, 1980).

CHAPTER 4

1. Schlesinger's remarks are in *Life*, November 1, 1948, pp. 65–66; Commager's are from *Parade*, May 8, 1977, pp. 16, 19.

2. Appendix 1, Section II, 4, 46. It is an interesting sidelight that the more conservative element among the survey historians on such personal moral matters also made up the bulk of those who believed a private school education was a better preparation for the presidency than a public education (see Appendix 1, Section II, 44).

3. For example, on a question pitting charisma against sincerity, more than 78 percent of the respondents preferred sincerity in a president to charisma. See Appendix 1, Section II, 5.

4. Appendix 1, Section III, Part A, 35; Part B, 36; Part C, 42.

5. Intelligence was consistently ranked the highest attribute, even above honesty. See Appendix 1, Section II, 62.

6. Appendix 1, Section III, Part C, 8.

7. Merle Miller, *Plain Speaking: An Oral Biography of Harry S. Truman* (New York: Berkeley Publishing Corp., 1974), quoting Sevareid, p. 402.

8. Appendix 1, Section III, Part C, 34, 38.

9. Appendix 1, Section II, 12, 43. In the latter instance, historians agreed with Richard Hofstadter, who claimed that no president could operate effectively without displaying some cunning. See Hofstadter, "The Right Man for the Big Job," p. 27.

10. Appendix 1, Section III, Part B, 2, and Section II, 56. A large minority (46 percent) did not believe a president should ever give out misleading information. Honesty clearly

remained one of the most highly prized traits, ranking just below intelligence in importance. See Appendix 1, Section II, 62.

11. Henry Steele Commager, "Yardstick for Presidential Candidates," *New York Times Magazine*, October 5, 1947, pp. 50–51, claimed that flexibility, as exemplified by FDR, was a crucial quality in a president.

12. Maranell, "The Evaluation of Presidents," pp. 104–113.

13. Miller, *Plain Speaking*, p. 344.

14. Richard Hofstadter, *The American Political Tradition and the Men Who Made It* (New York: Alfred A. Knopf, 1948), p. 207, quoting Theodore Roosevelt.

15. Appendix 1, Section II, 37; Section II, 2.

16. Appendix 1, Section III, Part C, 33, 36, 37. Determination and tenacity evidently had a slightly different connotation for most historians than aggressiveness. Aggressiveness was sometimes mentioned by the interviewees as a preferred attribute, but the mail survey historians ranked it much less in importance than some of the other attributes. See Appendix 1, Section II, 62.

17. Appendix 1, Section II, 21, and Section III, Part B, 14.

18. Jerald F. terHorst, *Gerald Ford and the Future of the Presidency* (New York: Third Press, 1974), p. 212.

19. Edward S. Corwin reached this same conclusion at the time of the first Schlesinger poll in 1948. See James Reston, "Qualities a President Needs," *New York Times Magazine*, October 31, 1948, p. 49, quoting Corwin.

20. For further statistical confirmation of this conclusion, see Simonton, "Presidential Greatness and Performance," pp. 306–323. For help in sorting out the relative statistical importance of these personality traits, we are indebted to Joshua P. Rosen and his fine honors paper, "Some Character Traits and Their Relation to Presidential Greatness" (The Pennsylvania State University, 1983).

CHAPTER 5

1. Cronin, *The State of the Presidency*, p. 251.

2. Appendix 1, Section II, 61.

3. Appendix 1, Section II, 13, 29; Section III, Part A, 32. For example, 89 percent declared that Polk justifiably dropped his famous campaign slogan of "54–40 or Fight" following his election in 1844.

4. Appendix 1, Section II, 17; Section III, Part B, 10, 23; Section III, Part C, 14.

5. Appendix 1, Section II, 31.

6. Louis W. Koenig, *The Chief Executive*, 3rd ed., (New York: Harcourt Brace Jovanovich, 1975), pp. 12–14.

7. Merle Miller, *Lyndon: An Oral Biography* (New York: Putnam and Sons, 1980), p. 277; Cronin, *State of the Presidency*, p. 220.

8. Appendix 1, Section II, 11; Section III, Part B, 34.

9. Appendix 1, Section II, 54.

10. Appendix 1, Section III, Part A, 27; Section III, Part B, 18.

11. Appendix 1, Section III, Part C, 4.

12. Appendix 1, Section III, Part B, 7.

13. Appendix 1, Section III, Part A, 18; Section II, 58.

14. Roger B. Porter, *Presidential Decision Making: The Economic Policy Board* (New York: Cambridge University Press, 1980), p. 18, quoting Dawes.

15. Cronin, *The State of the Presidency*, p. 186.

16. Appendix 1, Section II, 57. See also Appendix 1, Section III, 21, 36, 38. Some of this information was secured from the personal interviews.

17. Appendix 1, Section III, Part C, 2, 15.

18. Hugh Heclo, "The Changing Presidential Office," in Arnold J. Meltsner, ed., *Politics and the Oval Office* (New Brunswick, N.J.: Transaction Books, 1981), p. 179.

19. Appendix 1, Section II, 8, 18, 68, and material from interviewees. For examples of past presidents who were held accountable for the actions of cabinet officers, advisors, or friends, see Section III, Part B, 21, and Section III, Part C, 21.

20. David Brinkley, "Thirty Minutes with David Brinkley," PBS, July 13, 1971, statements by Truman and Johnson.

21. *New York Times*, November 13, 1932, quoting FDR.

22. Appendix 1, Section II, 61.

23. Appendix 1, Section III, Part C, 41.

24. One recent study has claimed that FDR *was* a first-rate administrator, contrary to FDR's own view. See A. J. Wann, *The President as Chief Administrator: A Study of Franklin D. Roosevelt* (Washington, D.C.: Public Affairs Press, 1968), esp. pp. 169–188.

25. CBS News Special (1973), "Five Presidents on the Presidency," interview with Truman; also Miller, *Plain Speaking*, p. 338.

26. Arthur M. Schlesinger, Jr., *Congress and the Presidency: Their Role in Modern Times* (Washington, D.C.: American Enterprise Institute for Public Policy Research, 1967), p. 4.

27. Appendix 1, Section II, 28.

28. Appendix 1, Section II, 19, 32.

29. Appendix 1, Section II, 39, 60.

30. Oral material from interviewed historians.

31. Appendix 1, Section II, 3, 34. Even in the case of Nixon, 85 percent of the survey historians agreed that he had the right to nominate and place on the Supreme Court justices who conformed to his socioeconomic views, including those on race and law and order. See Appendix 1, Section III, Part C, 22.

32. Appendix 1, Section II, 14; Section III, Part A, 17, 26; Section III, Part B, 19.

33. For a survey of presidential-media relationships, see William J. Small, *Political Power and the Press* (New York: W. W. Norton, 1972).

34. Ibid., p. 46.

35. Theodore Roosevelt is credited with starting the modern news conference, but he did not hold them regularly. Wilson scheduled them until 1915, when they were discontinued. Harding restored them, and his successor, Coolidge, followed along. Hoover cut them back drastically and demanded that questions be submitted by journalists in advance. It was FDR who initiated the "open" press conference as we now know it, with reporters on record asking questions from the floor. Truman continued this practice, and Eisenhower was the first to use television. For the statistics, see Appendix 1, Section II, 26, 56.

36. Appendix 1, Section II, 16, 42, 45.

37. Appendix 1, Section II, 40.

38. Appendix 1, Section III, Part A, 2, 21, and material from interviewees.

39. Appendix 1, Section III, Part C, 33, 34, 35, 39.

40. Small, *Political Power and the Press*, p. 56.

41. For the historians' attitude on presidential removals, see Appendix 1, Section III, Part B, 6, 12; Section III, Part C, 11, 29.

CHAPTER 6

1. Hofstadter, "The Right Man for the Big Job," p. 112, quoting Nevins.

2. James M. Burns, "The One Test," *New York Times Magazine*, May 1, 1980, p. 102, quoting Attlee.

3. Tugwell and Cronin, eds., *The Presidency Reappraised*, p. 171, quoting Gallup.

4. Gary M. Maranell and Richard A. Dodder, "Political Orientation and the Evaluation of Presidential Prestige: A Study of American Historians," *Social Science Quarterly*, no. 51 (September 1970), pp. 415–421.

5. See Appendix 1, Section III, Part A, 7, 8; Section III, Part C, 10, 20. See also Section III, 11, 14.

6. Appendix 1, Section II, 61, and material from oral interviews.

7. Arthur B. Tourtellot, *The Presidents on the Presidency* (New York: Russell and Russell, 1970), p. 122, quoting Hoover.

8. Appendix 1, Section II, 3. See also Section II, 25, and Section III, Part A, 10.

9. Appendix 1, Section III, Part C, 29; Section III, Part C, 4.

10. Appendix 1, Section III, Part A, 15, 16, 24, 25; Section III, Part B, 20, 28, 35; Section III, Part C, 33.

11. Appendix 1, Section II, 66. At the complete other end of the scale, 5 percent of the respondents said they approved of a president ordering the assassination of the leader of a domestic terrorist organization, if that would preserve national stability. See Appendix 1, Section II, 65.

12. One can conjecture that a partial reason for this has been a sharp increase in interest of American historians in new areas of inquiry that deeply involve civil rights, such as Afro-American history and women's history.

13. Appendix 1, Section III, Part A, 1, 10, 19, 30, 31; Section III, Part B, 22; see also Section II, 55.

14. Appendix 1, Section III, Part C, 14, 26, 33.

15. Appendix 1, Section III, Part C, 28.

16. Appendix 1, Section II, 53, 61, and oral material from interviews.

17. For example, see Henry S. Commager, "What Makes Presidential Greatness," *New York Times Magazine*, July 22, 1945, p. 37. For an interesting analysis and ranking of the presidents as "diplomats," see Elmer Plischke, "Rating Presidents and Diplomats in Chief," *Presidential Studies Quarterly*, vol. 15, no. 4 (Fall 1985), pp. 725–742; "Five Presidents on the Presidency," CBS News Special (1973), interviews with Truman, Eisenhower, and Nixon; Tugwell and Cronin, eds., *The Presidency Reappraised*, p. 235.

18. *Los Angeles Times*, September 9, 1973, quoting Kissinger.

19. Arthur M. Schlesinger, Jr., *The Imperial Presidency* (Boston: Houghton Mifflin, 1973), p. ix.

20. Material from oral interviews. See also Appendix 1, Section III, Part B, 5.

21. Appendix 1, Section II, 39.

22. For examples of pragmatism or expediency versus morality in foreign policy see Appendix 1, Section III, Part A, 33; Section III, Part C, 17, 23, 28, 31.

23. For example, a majority of the respondents believed a president should not order the assassination of an enemy of the United States even in wartime. See Appendix 1, Section II, 65.

24. For example, 73 percent of the historians disagreed with Theodore Roosevelt's unilateral activities in Latin America and 65 percent thought Congress should have prevented his "rape" of Panama. On the other hand, 68 percent agreed that he had the right to send out the fleet, even without congressional funding. See Appendix 1, Section III, Part B, 13, 27, 32.

25. Appendix 1, Section III, Part A, 5, 9, 12, 20; Section III, Part B, 8, 11, 17, 25, 33; Section III, Part C, 12, 16, 27, 30. The exceptions are Appendix 1, Section III, Part C, 1, 24. Is it possible that these two examples betrayed a Russophobic attitude on the part of these American historians? Admittedly, in the case of the Afghan rebels, the division was close—52 percent for sending aid, 48 percent against.

26. Appendix 1, Section II, 67.

27. Appendix 1, Section III, Part C, 9.

28. It is interesting that 75 percent of the respondents did not believe that Lincoln should be downgraded for his poor selection of generals in the early stages of the Civil War. The historians apparently assumed that, in Lincoln's case, all's well that ends well. See Appendix 1, Section III, Part A, 13.

29. For a general survey of all the presidents as commander-in-chief, see Warren W. Hassler, *The Presidents as Commander-in-Chief* (Menlo Park, Calif.: Addison-Wesley, 1971).

30. See Appendix 1, Section III, Part B, 1, 15. Although post−White House activities held no discernible importance for the Murray-Blessing historians in assigning the presidents a rank in history, these historians did display considerable interest in how the careers of former presidents were managed. To these historians, a person was permanently marked by the office, and even though he returned to private life he still remained "special." They believed that a former president could not, and should not, conduct his private affairs as if he had never held the position. The range of activities the survey historians thought proper for a former president was interesting. A large majority (82 percent) believed that it was proper for a former president to make money from his memoirs and other writings. Seventy-nine percent also endorsed the idea that a former president be paid for lectures and formal speaking engagements. A smaller 59 percent thought that it was suitable for him to receive money as a business consultant or director of a corporation. But only a bare majority (52 percent) agreed that he should earn money from television talk shows or interviews, and a scant 10 percent approved of a former president selling his name to endorse a commercial product. On the other hand, an overwhelming 97 percent supported the idea of a former president running for and holding public office again in some other position, even though only two presidents in history (John Q. Adams and Andrew Johnson) did so successfully. See Appendix 1, Section II, 69; Section III, Part A, 4.

31. Dean K. Simonton, a psychologist at the University of California (Davis) specializing in executive leadership, emphasized this theme in his *Genius, Creativity, and Leadership: Historiometric Inquiries* (Cambridge: Harvard University Press, 1984), p. 165. Said Simonton, "The impact of the situation . . . is tempered by . . . individual attributes. . . . 'Being the right person' is almost as important as 'being in the right place at the right time. . . .' A

certain type of genius may have a higher probability of accomplishment when the spirit of the times takes one form, whereas another type of genius may have an advantage when the zeitgeist shifts to another emphasis."

CHAPTER 7

1. See Bailey, *Presidential Greatness*, pp. 23–34.

2. These letters are in the possession of Robert K. Murray. For the *Parade* release, see Lloyd Shearer, "Intelligence Report: U.S. Presidents—How They Rate," *Parade Magazine*, December 12, 1982, p. 10.

3. These groupings were first brought to our attention by Murphy, "Evaluating the Presidents of the United States," draft of paper sent to Robert K. Murray.

4. For examples, see Appendix 1, Section III, Part B, 3, 9, 24. Although basically "liberal," the historians showed no particular bias against self-made or wealthy persons occupying the White House. On the other hand, they did not believe a wealthy person, per se, would make a better president than one from more modest circumstances. See Appendix 1, Section II, 38, 48.

5. Maranell and Dodder, "Political Orientation and the Evaluation of Presidential Prestige: A Study of American Historians," p. 418 and passim.

6. When the historians were asked to rank the nine most recent presidents on the basis of who practiced the most and the least "imperial" presidency, they placed their two lowest-ranked modern presidents at the top and at the bottom of their list, apparently affirming again that although they do not want a president who is too strong, they do not want a weak one either. See Appendix 1, Section III, Part C, 40.

7. Appendix 1, Section III, Part C, 32.

8. "In Elections We Deal with Choices, Not Absolutes," *Time*, September 15, 1980, p. 19, interview with Pat Caddell.

9. For the best analysis of these paradoxes, see Cronin, *The State of the Presidency*, 2nd. ed.

10. For the results of the various polls, see "Every Four Years," PBS, September 11, 1980, with Howard K. Smith; *Time*, November 19, 1984, p. 45; "The Mood of the Voter," *Time*, September 15, 1980, p. 8; November 12, 1984, p. 37.

11. *Public Papers of the President* (Washington, D.C., 1964), p. 815, quoting Kennedy.

12. See John Chancellor, "Those Presidential News Conferences—How to Make Them Better," *TV Guide*, May 14, 1983, pp. 4–7.

13. Bailey, *Presidential Greatness*, pp. 21–22, citing the Gallup poll.

14. George H. Gallup, ed., *The Gallup Poll, 1935–1971* (New York: Random House, 1972), p. 986.

15. *The Gallup Poll: Public Opinion, 1972–1977* (Wilmington, Del.: Scholarly Resources, 1978); vol. 2, p. 641.

16. Miller, *Plain Speaking*, p. 16.

17. "Five Presidents on the Presidency," CBS News Special, interview with Eisenhower.

18. Ibid., interviews with Truman, Eisenhower, Kennedy, Lyndon Johnson, and Nixon. See also "Every Four Years," PBS, with Howard K. Smith, interviews with Nixon, Ford, and Carter. See also Dwight D. Eisenhower, "Six Qualities that Make a President," *Time*, June 14, 1963, p. 28.

19. "Every Four Years," PBS, with Howard K. Smith, interviews with Ford, Nixon, and Carter.

20. "FDR: A Special Report," ABC Special, January 29, 1982, with David Brinkley, and comments on FDR by Nixon, Ford, Carter, and Reagan. For a stimulating book on the influence of FDR on subsequent presidents, see William R. Leuchtenburg, *In the Shadow of FDR: From Harry Truman to Ronald Reagan* (Ithaca: Cornell University Press, 1983).

CHAPTER 8

1. Indeed, three years after leaving the White House, Reagan was still much more controversial than Jimmy Carter was a year after his departure.

2. Cited in "Chronicle," *New York Times*, March 13, 1991, p. B6.

3. Alexander M. Haig, *Caveat: Realism, Reagan, and Foreign Policy* (New York: Macmillan Publishing Co., 1984), p. 85.

4. Donald T. Regan, *For the Record: From Wall Street to Washington* (New York: Harcourt Brace Jovanovich, 1988), passim, but note the telling remarks on pp. 188, 189, 377. Although Regan does say that Reagan should be considered a Great president, he leaves little doubt that his position on Reagan is one of intense ambivalence—above and beyond the bitterness he reveals concerning his own fate. Fred I. Greenstein, "Ronald Reagan—Another Hidden-Hand Ike?" *PS: Political Science and Politics*, vol. 23, no. 1 (March 1990), pp. 7–12.

5. David A. Stockman, *The Triumph of Politics: How the Reagan Revolution Failed* (New York: Harper and Row, 1986), passim. Perhaps the most critical book by someone around Reagan, surpassing even Donald Regan's in bitterness, this portrait of a befuddled Reagan could rightly be called devastating. See pp. 355–375 for an extraordinarily harsh sketch of an American president by an "insider."

6. Martin Anderson, *Revolution* (New York: Harcourt Brace Jovanovich, 1988), photo caption between pp. 138 and 139 and also p. 280; Larry Speakes with Robert Pack, *Speaking Out: The Reagan Presidency from Inside the White House* (New York: Charles Scribner's Sons, 1988), p. 114; Regan, *For the Record*, p. 271.

7. Bell, *The Thirteenth Man*, p. 31. For a balanced appraisal of Reagan's skills as president, see Richard P. Nathan, "The Presidency After Reagan: Don't Change It—Make It Work," in Larry Berman, ed., *Looking Back on the Reagan Presidency* (Baltimore: Johns Hopkins University Press, 1990), pp. 195–206.

8. Speakes, *Speaking Out*, p. 109; Regan, *For the Record*, p. 34; Ronald Reagan, *An American Life*, (New York: Simon and Schuster, 1990), p. 512; Jane Mayer and Doyle McManus, *Landslide: The Unmaking of the President* (Boston: Houghton Mifflin, 1988), p. 179.

9. Peggy Noonan, *What I Saw at the Revolution: A Political Life in the Reagan Era* (New York: Random House, 1990).

10. Anderson, *Revolution*, pp. 63–72; interview with Martin Anderson, February 24, 1991. For an analysis of Reagan's first inaugural, see Herbert W. Simons and Aram A. Aghazarian, eds., *Form, Genre, and the Study of Political Discourse* (Columbia: University of South Carolina Press, 1986), pp. 197–347.

11. American Historical Association, *Guide to Departments of History, 1986–1987: Col-*

leges, Universities, and Research Institutes in the United States and Canada (Washington, D.C.: AHA, 1988).

12. In order, the Murray-Blessing rankings of the presidents are as follows. *Great*—Lincoln, F. Roosevelt, Washington, Jefferson; *Near-Great*—T. Roosevelt, Wilson, Jackson, Truman; *Above Average*—J. Adams, L. Johnson, Eisenhower, Polk, Kennedy, Madison, Monroe, J. Q. Adams, Cleveland; *Average*—McKinley, Taft, Van Buren, Hoover, Hayes, Arthur, Ford, Carter, B. Harrison; *Below Average*—Taylor, Reagan, Tyler, Fillmore, Coolidge, Pierce; *Failure*—A. Johnson, Buchanan, Nixon, Grant, Harding. See Robert K. Murray and Tim H. Blessing, *Greatness in the White House: Rating the Presidents, Washington through Carter* (University Park, Pa.: The Pennsylvania State University Press, 1988), p. 16.

13. Anderson, *Revolution*, p. 176.

14. Reagan, *An American Life*, p. 401; see also pp. 149, 150.

15. Ibid., p. 280.

16. Tom Joe and Cheryl Rogers, *By the Few for the Few* (Lexington, Mass.: Lexington Books, 1985), introduction by Hale Champion, p. xiv.

17. Ibid., pp. 149–150.

18. Fifty-four percent condemn Reagan's support of the Contras in the strongest terms available.

19. As Dean Simonton, a psychologist specializing in the psychology of leadership, has noted, the interplay of scandal and the perception of an administration's worth is one of the strongest factors in establishing presidential rankings. See Dean Keith Simonton, "Personality and Politics," in Lawrence A. Pervin, ed., *Handbook of Personality: Theory and Research* (New York: Guilford Press, 1990), p. 682, in which Simonton indicates that scandal is the fourth most important factor in observers' perceptions of presidential rankings, behind years in office, number of war years, and assassination.

20. At the Reykjavik summit, 40 percent believed that Reagan should have accepted Gorbachev's offer of a grand settlement, almost 30 percent believed he should not have accepted Gorbachev's offer, and slightly more than 30 percent were unsure about what Reagan should have done.

21. The fact that Reagan was generally ready to accept half a loaf is a point made by several Reagan associates. Anderson, *Revolution*, pp. 241–242, 284–286, attributes this willingness to compromise to Reagan's background as a labor leader and the skills acquired in labor negotiations. Secretary of Education Terrell Bell, in a small book that has received too little notice, *The Thirteenth Man* (New York: The Free Press, 1988), indicates (p. 31) that Reagan's more fervid supporters may have been discomforted by Reagan's willingness to compromise. Reagan himself states that he and many conservatives parted company over his willingness to accept less than total victory (Reagan, *An American Life*, p. 171).

22. Varying from r = .57 to r = .79.

CONCLUSIONS

1. See Simonton, "Presidential Greatness and Performance," pp. 306–323; also Wendt and Light, "Measuring Greatness in American Presidents," pp. 105–109.

2. Ibid.; see also Simonton, "Presidential Greatness and Performance," pp. 306–323. Compare with Maranell, "The Evaluation of Presidents: An Extension of the Schlesinger Polls," pp. 104–113.

3. See James D. Barber, *The Pulse of Politics: Electing Presidents in the Media Age* (New York: W. W. Norton, 1980).

4. James D. Barber, *The Presidential Character: Predicting Performance in the White House* (Englewood Cliffs, N.J.: Prentice-Hall, 1972).

5. Reston, "Qualities a President Needs," p. 47, quoting Wilson.

6. Hedley Donovan, "The Enigmatic President," *Time*, May 6, 1985, p. 24, quoting Johnson.

7. Tourtellot, *The Presidents on the Presidency*, p. 422, quoting Theodore Roosevelt.

8. Truman once said, "One of the reasons for reading history is to learn from it and, if possible, make use of it." Miller, *Plain Speaking*, p. 324.

9. See Appendix 1, Section II, 59. It is interesting that, of the various inputs making a presidential image, the historians ranked White House public relations the least effective.

10. If we rigidly applied some of the "predictors" mentioned earlier in these conclusions, Washington, John Adams, John Q. Adams, Monroe, and Polk all would have been poor choices. The most successful president in the late nineteenth century (Cleveland) also would not have made it. See Simonton, "Presidential Greatness and Performance," table on p. 316.

11. For a synopsis of the criticisms of the "textbook" presidency as exemplified by FDR, see Malcolm G. Scully, "Political Scientists Criticize Research on Presidency," *Chronicle of Higher Education*, September 14, 1983, pp. 7–8.

12. Ibid., quoting Greenstein. For his book on Eisenhower, see Fred I. Greenstein, *The Hidden Hand Presidency: Eisenhower as Leader* (New York: Basic Books, 1982).

13. See Appendix 1, Section II, 49, 50. In a recent public opinion poll, 40 percent of 1,500 respondents believed that a Jew might be elected by the year 2000, 37 percent thought that an African-American might, but only 33 percent believed a woman would. These public opinion statistics are from "Every Four Years," PBS, with Howard K. Smith.

14. James Bryce, *The American Commonwealth* (New York: Commonwealth Publishing Co., 1908), vol. 1, p. 91. See especially Chapter 8, pp. 84–92, on "Why Great Men Are Not Chosen Presidents."

15. George E. Reedy, *The Twilight of the Presidency* (New York: World Publishing Co., 1970).

16. Harold M. Barger, *The Impossible Presidency: Illusions and Realities of Executive Power* (Glenview, Ill.: Scott, Foresman and Company, 1984), pp. 2, 3.

17. It might be argued that this represents circular reasoning. But if this is merely circular, then the exceptions of Lincoln, Grant, and Nixon remain to be explained. Also, there were other two-term presidents who were considered neither Great nor Near Great and were not ranked very high (e.g., Cleveland, seventeenth).

18. The mean average ranking for presidents Washington through John Q. Adams was 2.37; for FDR through Carter, 3.31; for Theodore Roosevelt through Hoover, 3.34; for Lincoln through McKinley, 3.92; and for Jackson through Buchanan, 4.14. Reagan's ranking was determined after this compilation was made.

19. Morton Borden, ed., *America's Ten Greatest Presidents* (Chicago: Rand McNally, 1961), p. 3, quoting Hamilton.

20. Cronin, *The State of the Presidency*, p. 2.

Index